RUSSIA

Jon Nichol and Keith Shephard

GENERAL EDITOR **Jon Nichol**

Contents

Basil Blackwell

1 Russia in 1900

How are we ruled? Do we live in a democracy or an *autocracy* – a state in which one man governs? In 1900 the ruler of Russia, Tsar Nicholas II (1894–1917), was an autocrat. When he became Tsar in 1894 Nicholas had little idea of how to run Russia. Shy and weak-willed, he was under the thumb of his German wife, Alexandra (**A**).

As Russia's autocrat Nicholas had total power. He could make laws by himself, as Russia had no parliament. Nicholas picked ministers himself. Often they were close friends, drawn from his court circle. How did Nicholas rule? To carry out his orders he relied on:

- *the army* – its officers were mainly nobles.
- *the secret police* – who jailed anyone who spoke out or plotted against the Tsar.
- *the civil service* – a huge, inefficient body which collected taxes and governed the provinces.
- *the aristocrats* – who owned vast estates, where lived the bulk of Russia's population, the peasants.

Nicholas made many mistakes. But he had a hard job to do. Russia in 1900 was changing fast. Nicholas faced many difficult problems.

Russia was a backward country when compared with other European countries like Germany and Britain. The population, which was growing quickly, could not

A Nicholas and Alexandra in 1898

B Living conditions for a Russian peasant family

be fed easily. Farming methods were like those used in the Middle Ages. Most of Russia's 130 million people – some 80 out of 100 – were peasants. Only 40 years before, in 1861, they had been freed from *serfdom*, a form of slavery.

Most peasants could not read or write. Home was usually a one-room wooden shack (see **B**). Smoke from the stove blackened the walls inside. The floor was the peasants' only bed except in winter when they might sleep on top of the stove. Common food was coarse black bread and cabbage soup. A police report of 1905 described the peasants' lifestyle:

‘Very often the peasants do not have enough allotment land, and cannot during the year feed themselves, clothe themselves, heat their homes, keep their tools and livestock, secure seed for sowing and lastly discharge (pay) all their taxes . . .’ (C)

By 1900 many peasants were leaving the countryside to work in factories in the towns. There were few factories until the last ten years of the nineteenth century. Then Russia began to build large factories. Industry made twice as much in 1900 as in 1890. Towns grew very quickly, especially Moscow and St Petersburg. Large slums grew up in these towns to house the factory workers.

Life for the workers was very hard. In cotton factories many of them had coffin-like boxes between the machines, where they slept in filth. One woman worker in a rope factory wrote:

‘There was no dawdling here – the slightest carelessness could end in tragedy: I myself saw a youth lose three fingers in an instant. We workers ate and drank our tea sitting on dirty coils of rope; after dinner, we curled up on them like kittens and slept. No one brought dinner to the factory: we simply bought chunks of lard and olives and white bread at the factory gate and took turns to bring boiling water from the tavern.’ (D)

Other workers lived in rooms near the factories. Several families usually shared one room, which was divided up by curtains or wooden partitions. Official reports of 1902 described rooms which were:

‘. . . damp and unbelievably dirty. In two rooms there is complete darkness. The ceiling is so low that a tall man cannot stand upright . . . the plaster is crumbling, there are holes in the walls stopped up with rags. It is dirty. The stove has collapsed. Legions of cockroaches and bugs. No double window frames and so it is piercingly cold. The lavatory is so dilapidated that it is dangerous to enter and children are not allowed in . . . in rainy weather water on the floor is two inches deep.’ (E)

F shows a corner of a room which was home for two families at the Putilov Steel Works in St Petersburg.

The badly paid factory workers worked long hours and lived in foul conditions. This led to strikes, riots and hatred of their bosses.

In 1900 Russia had a small middle class – 3 per cent of the population. It consisted of people like civil servants, factory and shop owners, merchants, lawyers, doctors and teachers. Many wanted a share in government. They wanted a parliament to make laws; free speech and press; an end to the secret police and freedom to meet and talk. They too were a problem that Nicholas had to solve.

F Each family rented a corner of this room in St Petersburg

??????????????????

1 Use the map inside the back cover to draw your own map of Russia. Mark on it the Trans-Siberian Railway, the Ural Mountains, Moscow and St Petersburg. Measure Russia's widest point (E – W). How long would it take to cross it: on horse (travelling at 30 miles a day); by train (at 300 miles a day)?

2 a What type of ruler is an *autocrat*?
b Why was Russia a backward country in 1900?
c In what ways was Russia changing by 1900?

3 The police report of 1905 (**C**) describes how the peasants lived. Use **B** and the text to help you write two further paragraphs for the report, about the peasants and their homes.

4 a F shows a room similar to the description in **E**, the Official Report of 1902. List the parts of the description in the Report which could apply to this room.
b Make a list of five complaints about living in the room that the girl sitting on the right might make.

5 If you were an advisor to the Tsar in 1900, what advice would you give him to help solve his problems?

2 The Revolutionaries

A Karl Marx (1818–83)

The foul conditions in which workers and peasants lived led to strikes and riots. The Tsar used his secret police, the *Okhrana*, to control and arrest his enemies. More and more *revolutionaries* wanted to get rid of the Tsar. There were two revolutionary groups. The Social Revolutionary Party was formed in 1902. They believed that the peasants would start a revolution and should use force to bring down the Tsar. The other group, the Social Democratic Party, thought that the factory workers would bring about the revolution.

The Social Democrats believed in the ideas of a nineteenth century political thinker called Karl Marx (**A**). Marx set out his main ideas in *The Communist Manifesto* and *Das Kapital* (Capital). He saw history as a fight between the 'haves' and the 'have-nots'. The 'haves' owned land, mines, businesses or factories. The 'haves' kept the 'have-nots' under control and forced them to work in bad conditions for low wages. Among the 'haves' were the middle-class factory owners whom Marx called *capitalists*. These capitalists used the workers to make large profits. Marx called the workers the *proletariat*. The proletariat would become poorer until they rebelled against their capitalist bosses and seized control of all land, factories, mines and forests (**B**). We call these ideas of Marx *Communism*.

❛ *The immediate aim of the Communists is the . . . formation of the proletariat into a class, overthrow of the bourgeois (middle-class) supremacy, conquest of political power . . . The proletariat will use its political supremacy to wrest all capital from the bourgeoisie, to centralise all instruments of production in the hands of the state.* ❜ (**B**)

(Karl Marx *The Communist Manifesto*)

Marx said that workers' revolutions would occur in the industrial countries of Western Europe, not in Russia, where the working-class was too small. By 1903, however, the number of industrial workers in Russia was growing quickly. Workers still made up only a small part of the total population but Russian factories were large and employed many people. For example, the Putilov Steel Works in Petrograd employed thousands of men.

In 1903 the leading members of the Social Democratic Party met in London. But they argued about who should lead the party, and what it should do. At last they split into two groups: the *Bolsheviks* (greater or majority group) and the *Mensheviks* (lesser or minority group).

Lenin

Vladimir Ulyanov, better known as Lenin, was born in 1870. His father was a teacher and the family was comfortably-off. Lenin did well at school. His headmaster wrote in his report:

❛ *Very gifted, always neat and industrious, Ulyanov was first in all subjects and . . . received the gold medal as the most deserving pupil in ability, progress and conduct . . . Religion and discipline were the basis of* (his) *upbringing.* ❜ (**C**)

In 1887 Lenin's brother Alexander was hanged, along with four friends, for plotting to kill the Tsar. Lenin went to university a few months later. In December he was arrested for taking part in a student protest. Lenin, like his brother, now believed in the ideas of Karl Marx. The police now wrote a very different report on Lenin.

❛ *He attracted attention by his secretiveness, inattentiveness, and indeed rudeness. Two days before the riotous assembly he gave grounds for suspecting that he was meditating some improper behaviour . . . In view of the exceptional circumstances of the Ulyanov family, such behaviour . . . gave reason to believe him fully capable of unlawful and criminal demonstrations of all kinds.* ❜ (**D**)

Lenin was thrown out of university. He now spent his time studying the ideas of Marx and organising opposition to the Tsar's government. The Okhrana arrested Lenin and he spent a year in prison. Then he was sent for three years to the cold north-western part of Russia, called Siberia. After this he left Russia for London where he worked as editor of the revolutionary paper *Iskra* (The Spark). He was now a leading member of the Social Democratic Party and in 1903 attended the meeting of the Party in London. It was Lenin who helped cause the split of the Social Democratic Party and who emerged as leader of the Bolsheviks.

3 The Russian–Japanese War

The Tsar's problems grew worse between 1900 and 1904. Bad harvests and low wages led to peasant risings and workers' strikes. Even many of the middle and upper classes complained about the Tsar and wanted more say in how the country was run. Some joined the *Kadet* (Constitutional Democrats) *Party* which wanted the election of a parliament to help the Tsar rule. Some of the Tsar's ministers, like Plehve, feared there would be a revolution. They believed a short, victorious war was needed to make people forget the problems and to unite them behind the Tsar.

8 February 1904 Japan made a surprise attack on the Russian naval base at Port Arthur. This meant war. The cause of the quarrel was Chinese land. The Chinese Empire was falling apart and both Russia and Japan wanted parts of it. Russia had taken over Chinese Manchuria and Japan controlled Korea.

Most Russians welcomed the war. The Russian army, however, had problems. It is difficult to fight a war at a distance. Troops and supplies had to be sent on a six-day journey across Russia on the single track Trans-Siberian Railway (see **A**). The Japanese had shorter lines of supply. An army needs to be well run, but Russian organisation was bad. One officer waited weeks for ammunition. When a train did arrive he was horrified to find it brought gifts from the Tsar to the men — religious *icons* (pictures).

Another problem was that the Russian Pacific Fleet was shut up in Port Arthur. The Japanese laid seige to the Port and captured it in January 1905. At the end of February 1905 the main Japanese and Russian armies met at Mukden. Two weeks of hard fighting ended with a Japanese victory. The Russian Baltic Fleet left Europe to sail half-way round the world to help the Pacific Fleet. After an eight-month journey the ships steamed into the Straits of Tsushima in 1905 (see **A**). The Japanese Admiral Togo attacked with his faster and better-armed battle fleet. In under an hour most of the Russian ships were sunk or captured. Only three out of 27 ships escaped. The battle of Tsushima was a staggering defeat for Russia.

Both sides now wanted peace. The USA arranged the Treaty of Portsmouth (a town in New Hampshire, USA). Russia lost Port Arthur and much of Manchuria. Possibly the real importance of the war is the effect it had on the Russian people, as the next section shows.

A The Russo–Japanese War, 1904–5

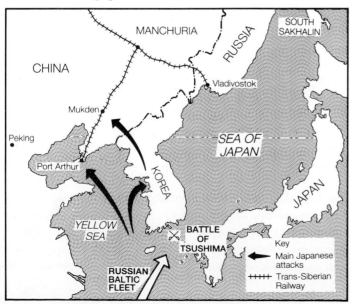

??????????????????

1 a How did the Tsar control strikes?
b How did the Social Revolutionaries and the Social Democrats differ?
c Why did Plehve want war?

2 Was Marx right? Copy out the table below and tick whether you agree or disagree with each idea. Compare your answers with a friend's.

	Agree	Disagree
1 History is a struggle between 'haves' and 'have-nots'		
2 The capitalists use the proletariat to make money		
3 In the end the proletariat always rebel		
4 Workers' revolutions will occur in all industrialised countries		

3 a What points in **C** suggest Lenin would be a good leader? Why?
b What do you think the writer of **D** meant by 'the exceptional circumstances of the Ulyanov family'?

4 In pairs, as if you were advising the Tsar, draw up your own plans for fighting the Japanese in 1905. Discuss these, then say:
a Why did the Russians choose their plans?
b Why might they have failed?

4 The 1905 Revolution

A Father Gapon

C An artist's view of Father Gapon and the marchers approaching the Winter Palace

January 1905 The war with Japan led to problems at home in Russia. The poor living conditions of peasants and factory workers had become even worse. Food was short, wages were low and prices were rising. People were angry at Russia's defeats. News of the fall of Port Arthur led to more strikes and unrest. Revolutionary groups like the Bolsheviks wanted to get rid of the Tsar. Other groups blamed his ministers and wanted a parliament to help the Tsar run the country.

In St Petersburg the police had, in secret, set up a trade union to control factory workers. A young priest, Father Gapon, led the union (**A**). He wanted to improve working conditions. He organised a strike and then a march of workers to present a *petition* (a list of requests) to the Tsar, asking for help. The petition began,

❝*Sire, we workers and our wives, children and helpless old parents, have come to you, our ruler, to seek justice and protection. We have become beggars . . . We are treated not as human beings, but as slaves. We have reached that awful moment when death is better than the continuation of unbearable suffering.* ❞ (**B**)

The petition then asked for better working conditions, a parliament chosen by the people and an end to the war. On Sunday 22 January Gapon and the marchers entered the square in front of the Tsar's Winter Palace

(**C**). They did not know the Tsar had left the day before. They sang hymns and the national anthem. A young man, Alexander Kerensky, watched the march. He wrote:

❝*It was an amazing sight. From the direction of the working-class districts came row upon row of orderly workers, all dressed in their best clothes. Gapon marched in front carrying a cross and a number of workers were holding pictures of the Tsar.* ❞ (**D**)

This was the beginning of what came to be called 'Bloody Sunday'. Gapon described what happened next:

❝*Suddenly the company of Cossacks (soldiers) galloped rapidly towards us with drawn swords. So then, it was to be a massacre after all. There was no time for giving orders. A cry of alarm arose as the Cossacks came down upon us. Our front ranks broke before them, opening to right and left, and down this lane the soldiers drove their horses, striking on both sides. I saw the swords lifting and falling, the men, women and children dropping to the earth like logs of wood, while moans, curses and shouts filled the air . . . Without any warning the dry crack of many rifle-shots was heard . . . I turned to the crowd and shouted to them to lie down . . . another volley was fired, and another, and yet another.* **)** (E)

The official report of events was different:

(*Gapon . . . excited the workers. In some places bloody clashes took place between workers and troops because of the stubborn refusal of the crowd to obey the command to go home, and sometimes even because of attacks upon the troops.* **)** (F)

G is an artist's impression of the events of 22 January. Reports of how many died differ greatly. The official figure was 96, but it was probably many more than this. A wave of strikes followed. The real revolution of 1905 was just beginning (see **H**). Unrest grew in the following months.

In St Petersburg and then in other towns the workers elected their own councils called *Soviets* to organise the strikes and run the towns. Something had to be done. Tsar Nicholas explained the problem to his mother:

(*There were only two ways open: to find an energetic soldier to crush the rebellion by sheer force. There would be time to breathe then, but likely as not one would have to use force again in a few months, and that would mean rivers of blood and in the end we should be where we started. The other way would be to give the people their civil rights, freedom of speech and press, also to have all laws agreed by a Duma (Parliament).* **)** (J)

G Bloody Sunday: the Cossacks attack

H Timechart: the 1905 Revolution

February	The Tsar's uncle, Grand Duke Sergei, was assassinated.
March	Peasant riots increased.
June	The crew of the battleship *Potemkin* mutinied in the port of Odessa. This led to street fighting in which 2000 people died. One sailor explained: *'We were forced to eat rotten biscuits and stinking decaying meat while our officers had the best food and drank the most expensive wines.'*
September	Printers went on strike.
October	A General Strike – railways, factories, mines, banks, law courts, shops, public transport and even the ballet all closed down.

Nicholas took the advice of his new minister, Witte, and agreed to the 'October Manifesto' (a list of changes). This gave the people freedom of speech and an elected Duma. It did nothing for the peasants and factory workers.

The workers' Soviets in St Petersburg and Moscow thought the Duma was worthless. They tried to close the factories through more strikes. But many middle-class people wanted to give the Duma a chance. The government quickly crushed the strikes. The revolution was over, but at least the people had the Duma, which many believed would share power with the Tsar. The Tsar did not agree.

??????????????

1 Explain the terms: Potemkin; Soviets; October Manifesto; Duma.

2 a Find evidence from **B** and **D** to show: that the march was meant to be peaceful; what the marchers thought of the Tsar.
b How do **E** and **F** differ about what happened? Why?

3 a What impression of the events of 1905 do you think the artist of **G** wanted to give?
b How reliable is **G** as evidence about the march?
c What kinds of secondary sources are there on this page? How useful do you think they are as evidence about the march?

4 You visit St Petersburg on 23 January 1905. First you ask a marcher (in **C**) and then a soldier (**G**) what has happened. Write about your conversations with each of them.

5 Describe what happened in the 1905 Revolution. How did the Tsar manage to stay in power?

5 Russian Politics, 1906–14

❝One saw peasants in their long coats, priests, Tartars, Poles, men in every kind of dress. Dignified old men, "intelligents" with long hair, a Polish bishop dressed in purple; men without collars, members of the proletariat, men in loose Russian shirts with belts and men dressed in costume of two centuries ago.❞ (A)

This is how one eyewitness described the first Duma which met in April 1906. One of Nicholas' ministers compared the Duma to:

❝. . . a gang of criminals who are only waiting for a signal to throw themselves upon the ministers and cut their throats. What wicked faces.❞ (B)

Nicholas believed he was appointed by God to rule. He did not want to share power with these different classes. So, as Tsar, he kept the right to dissolve (end) the Duma and did so in July 1906 when it demanded changes.

The second Duma met in March 1907 and was dissolved in June. Nicholas then changed the voting laws to make the vote of one landlord worth that of

C Peter Stolypin

D Stolypin's reforms

1 He improved education and conditions in the army and navy.
2 He promoted the building of factories and railways.
3 He encouraged peasants to leave the *Mir* (village community) and swop scattered strips of land for a farm in one block of land.
4 He encouraged richer peasants to buy out poorer peasants and set up bigger and more modern farms.

nearly 300 peasants or 600 workers. The next Duma backed the Tsar and it lasted its full term of five years. The fourth Duma also lasted five years.

In between the first and second Dumas, Nicholas made Peter Stolypin Prime Minister (C). Stolypin began to reform Russia. D shows some of these reforms.

Stolypin wanted to create a class of richer peasants, or *Kulaks*, who would support the Tsar's government and not want further political change. But according to Lenin, leader of the Bolsheviks, many poorer peasants suffered as a result:

❝The well-to-do peasants, the Kulaks, by leaving the Mir and buying up the allotments of the poor, are undoubtedly enriching themselves at other people's expense and ruining the masses. The vast majority of peasants are poor, they live like beggars and finally become homeless tramps. They live in dugouts, herding together with their cattle, starving, with sick and ragged children.❞ (E)

Stolypin's other aim was to crack down on the revolutionaries and strikers. Special courts were set up, and between 1906 and 1909 over 3000 people were executed. The hangman's noose became known as 'Stolypin's necktie'. Thousands of people were arrested and sent to Siberia. In some villages every tenth man was flogged as a warning.

Stolypin made many enemies – among the rich as well as the poor. Even the Tsar and Tsarina turned against him after he had quarrelled with the new court favourite, Gregory Rasputin. In September 1911 Stolypin was assassinated at the opera house in Kiev.

??????????????????

1 Make notes on: Kulaks; the Mir; 'Stolypin's necktie'.

2 Which people in **A** would the Tsar *least* have wanted to share power with? Give reasons for your answer.

3 a List Stolypin's reforms (**D**) in what you think is their order of importance. Explain why you chose that order.
 b As if you were a government supporter in 1912, write a speech to the Duma backing Stolypin's reforms.

4 a What does **E** tell us about Lenin's views of Stolypin's reforms?
 b How could you test whether these views were true?

6 War and Revolution

1914 August War broke out in Europe. Russia and her allies Britain and France faced Germany and Austria–Hungary.

Throughout Russia, most people were in favour of the war 'For Faith, Tsar and Country'. Love of Russia matched their fear and hatred of the Germans. A peasant told an ex-Prime Minister:

If we are unlucky enough not to destroy the Germans, they'll come here. They'll reign over the whole of Russia and then they'll harness you and me – yes, you as well as me – to their ploughs. (A)

Bruce Lockhart, a Briton living in Moscow at the time, tells us:

The heart of Russia was on fire with war . . . I see again those moving scenes at the station: the troops, grey with dust and closely packed in cattle trucks; the vast crowds on the platform to wish them God-speed . . . The wives of the rich merchants vied with each other in spending money on hospitals. There were gala performances at the State theatres in aid of the Red Cross. There was an orgy of national anthems. Every night at the opera and the ballet the Imperial orchestra played the national hymns of Russia, England, France and Belgium, while the audience stood at attention. (B)

A few Russians feared the war might end the Tsar's rule over Russia. Rasputin sent Nicholas a telegram:

Let Papa (his name for the Tsar) *not plan war, for with war will come the end of Russia and yourselves and you will lose to the last man.* (C)

Angrily, the Tsar tore up Rasputin's message. Within three years Rasputin's prophecy had proved true. In March 1917 Tsar Nicholas fell from power.

Why did the Tsar fall?

The rest of this section looks at some evidence about Russia between 1914 and 1917. We can use it to try and work out the reasons for the Tsar's downfall.

Table **D** lists the main events of the war. It shows that the Russians were able to defeat the armies of Austria–Hungary but suffered heavy defeats from the German forces.

E on page 10 shows eight reasons or *factors* that may have led to the overthrow of the Tsar. You can find out more about each of them on the next pages. (You might want to add to this list as you find out more about the events of March 1917.)

D Timechart: August 1914 – January 1917

1914

August Outbreak of war. Russia's armies prepare to attack Germany.

25–30 August Battle of Tannenberg. Heavy defeat of one of two main Russian armies by Germans.

7–14 September Second Russian army driven out of East Germany at Battle of the Masurian Lakes. German commanders Hindenberg and Ludendorff given credit for major victories. Russian armies reform and counter-attack Galicia. Austrians lose half their troop – 400 000 men.

Winter Fighting continues on North-Western Front against Germans and in Galicia against Austrians. Limited German advances. Failure of German winter campaign. Russian victories over Austrians on Galician Front.

1915

May–September Major German successes on North-Western Front and in Galicia. Russians retreat. (Quality of German command and use of artillery crucial factors. The well-equipped but poorly trained Russian army failed in the Spring Offensives partly because it mis-used its artillery units.)

1916

June Brusilov new Russian commander in Galicia. Has young, well-trained officers, copies German methods of attack. Major victories over Austrian army by *mid-July*. Russian army well-equipped with rifles, machine-guns, artillery and shells – Russian 'war machine' fully able to equip forces.

Summer Failure of Russian armies on North-Western Front – stalemate.

August–October Brusilov fails to defeat remaining Austrian forces – stalemate.

August Romania declares war on Austria and Germany. Russian and Romanian armies collapse – increasing danger of Austrian attack in the south.

1917

January Although still well-equipped fighting forces, Russian armies driven out of Poland and Romania.

E Reasons why the Tsar fell from power

1 *The Tsar's role as commander-in-chief* From August 1915 the Tsar in person was in charge of the army at the front. How much was he blamed for the army's failure? Was it felt that his removal would allow the war to be fought with more success?

2 *The role of the Tsarina, Alexandra* With the Tsar at the front, the government was in the hands of Alexandra. How important was hatred of her for being a German? Were feelings that she was working for Germany a factor in causing the Tsar to fall?

3 *The role of Rasputin* Rasputin is the Russian word for 'dissolute'. Rasputin was the Tsarina's chief adviser. What part did Russians' loathing of Rasputin play in the collapse of support for the Tsar?

4 *The collapse of government* By early 1917 the government was a shambles. Did people want to replace the Tsar's government with one which would run the country better?

5 *The economy* Shortage of food and high prices meant workers were ready to riot against the government. How did this lead to its fall?

6 *The collapse of support for the war* By early 1917 support for the war was ending. How important was the Tsar's wish to go on fighting to the bitter end in losing him vital support?

7 *The state of the army* How far did mutinies and a feeling of despair among the generals, army officers and troops contribute to the collapse of support for the Tsar?

8 *The role of the Duma* Did the Tsar's refusal to co-operate with the Duma, and use its backing, lead to the loss of political support in Petrograd?

F Tsar Nicholas at the front – holding up an icon before kneeling soldiers

Factor 1 The Tsar as commander of the army

In August 1915 the Tsar took over in person as commander of the army, and went to live at the front (**F**). His ministers and Rodzianko, president of the Duma, warned him that this might be a fatal mistake. They said he would be linked with any failure of the army (see *Factor 8*). In January 1917 a general talked to the Duma about feelings among the army's generals:

❝*The feeling in the army is such that all will greet with joy the news of a coup d'etat* (an uprising to remove the Tsar).❞ (**G**)

The generals felt that unless the Tsar was removed there could be no victory.

Factor 2 The role of the Empress, Alexandra

With Nicholas at the front, Alexandra took charge of the government. Russians hated her because she was a German and because of the hold Rasputin had over her (see *Factor 3*). Bruce Lockhart kept a diary during his stay in Moscow. An entry for 1915 said:

❝*Today an officer telephoned to ask when England was going to rid Russia of "the German woman". This, of course, was a reference to the Empress, and my own comment was: "This is the third time that this kind of thing has happened this week." To this period, too, belongs the most popular Moscow story of the war. The Tsarevitch (the Tsar's son Alexis) is seen crying in the corridor of the Winter Palace. A general, who is leaving the Palace after an audience, stops and pats the boy's head.*
"What is wrong, my little man?"
"When the Russians are beaten, papa cries. When the Germans are beaten, mama cries. When am I to cry?"❞ (**H**)

Factor 3 The role of Rasputin

Rasputin was a peasant from Siberia who became a *starets* or Holy Man. In 1905 in St Petersburg he was introduced to Tsar Nicholas' family. Soon Rasputin gained a hold over Nicholas and Alexandra. His power came from his ability to heal their son and heir, Alexis, who suffered from haemophilia (this meant his blood would not clot). If Alexis hurt himself, Rasputin could stop the boy bleeding to death. By 1914 Rasputin was infamous for his influence at court. He made love to many members of the royal circle (**J**). He was often drunk and took part in wild orgies.

From August 1915 Rasputin gained a new role. He became Alexandra's chief adviser. The extracts in **K** come from messages to Tsar Nicholas from Alexandra. They suggest how Rasputin helped choose ministers, and played a part in planning battles:

❝*. . . Forgive me, but I don't like the choice of Minister of War Polivanov. Is he not our Friend's (Rasputin's) enemy?* (Polivanov was an outstanding military organiser. He fell on 25 March 1916.)
25 July 1916 Our Friend . . . finds it better not to advance too obstinately as the losses will be too great. (In August 1916 the Tsar halted the Brusilov offensive, see **D**.)❞ (**K**)

By December 1916 Duma members and many nobles were certain that Rasputin was a German agent and that

J Rasputin at court, surrounded by society ladies

he had wrecked the Russian government on purpose. On 30 December Prince Yusupov murdered Rasputin. He fed him poisoned cakes and wine. When they did not work, Yusupov shot him with a pistol. Still Rasputin lived. Finally he was bundled up in a coat and shoved through a hole in the ice on the River Neva. When Rasputin's corpse was found, it was discovered that he had drowned.

Factor 4 The collapse of government

In August 1915 the cabinet of ministers told the Tsar that they could not back his plan to take over command of the army and leave the running of the government to the Empress. With Alexandra and Rasputin in charge of ministers at St Petersburg, from August 1915 to February 1917, Russia had four prime ministers, five ministers of the interior, four ministers of agriculture and three ministers of war.

Bribery and corruption were rampant. The government was in a state of chaos. Food, guns, ammunition and clothing failed to reach the army. Food was scarce in the towns. In March 1916, Rodzianko tells us:

In Petrograd there was a shortage of meat, but those passing through the city could see a string of carts, loaded with rotting carcasses which were being taken to the soap factory . . . This meat was intended for the army, but there was no place to keep

it . . . Permission and money for new cold storage plants has been refused. Ministries did not co-operate. An official ordered the meat, the railways brought it, but there was no place to store it . . . (L)

In December 1917 General Ruzski, commander of the Northern Front, commented:

The Northern Front does not receive even its meat allowance . . . We lack internal organisation. (M)

Factor 5 The economy

In 1915 Russia was a poor country when compared to Germany or Britain. Relative to their size, for each mile of Russian railway there were ten German miles. For every Russian factory, Britain had 150. By December 1916, Russia's railways were so badly run that not enough food could be moved from grain-growing areas to the town. Food queues like **N** were common in Petrograd. Prices rose sharply during the war, as **O** shows.

O Price rises 1913–17

	1913	100
	1915	130
January	1916	155
January	1917	300
October	1917	755

N A bread queue in Petrograd

In February 1917 Bruce Lockhart commented:

the storm broke, and in a night a bread-riot, similar to hundreds which had taken place during the previous 12 months, had become a revolution . . . It was a bitterly cold day. Our house, which was central-heated, had been short of fuel for nearly a week. **(P)**

The growth of the army **(Q)** had placed a great strain on the economy. By 1916 strikes were widespread in the factories of Moscow and Petrograd.

Q The growth of the army 1914–17

	1914	1915	1916	mid 1917
Number of men in armed forces (millions)	6.5	11.2	14.2	15.1
Percentage of men of working age	15%	25%	36%	37%

During the war the Russian economy grew very quickly. In 1916 it made enough guns and ammunition for the Russian army to be fully equipped:

There was 2000 per cent growth in output of shells, 1000 per cent in artillery, 1100 per cent in rifles. Four Russian factories . . . produced 80 per cent of the monthly 222 aircraft Russia was said to need in 1915–16 . . . The army's 10000 telephones became 50000 in 1916. Artillery showed the advance best . . . The Russian figure for 1917 (1 January) is actually higher than the French one for August 1916, and is well over double the British one for that month. **(R)**

(N Stone, *The Eastern Front* 1976)

Factor 6 The collapse of support for the war

In December 1916 Bruce Lockhart was in St Petersburg:

Champagne flowed like water. The Astoria and the Europe – the two best hotels in the capital – were thronged with officers who should have been at the Front. There was no disgrace in being a "shirker" or in finding a soft job in the rear. **(S)**

Bruce Lockhart thought that the March 1917 revolution broke out because:

the patience of the Russian people broke down under a system of unparalleled inefficiency and corruption . . . As examples of the inefficiency, I give the disgraceful handling of food supplies, the complete breakdown of transport . . . **(T)**

Factor 7 The state of the army

The Russian army of 1914 had been mainly trained to fight using the charge – cavalry with sabers (a type of sword), infantry with bayonets. Facing them were German troops with machine guns and plenty of field and heavy artillery. Each German division had twice as many field guns as a Russian division, and the Germans had 381 divisions of heavy guns compared with the 60 Russian divisions. German troops had full supplies of ammunition and rifles, Russian forces were short of both. The Russians were dug in in shallow trenches **(U)** while the Germans had deep and solid fortifications.

In May 1915 the German attack in Poland smashed the Russian armies; half the army was destroyed. 1 400 000 fell in battle or were wounded, 976 000 became prisoners. German field guns pounded the Russians to bits, as General Deniken reported:

The German heavy guns swept away whole lines of trenches,

U A dugout on the Russian Front

and their defenders with them. We hardly replied – there was nothing with which we could reply. Our regiments . . . beat off one attack after another by bayonet . . . Blood flowed unendingly. **(V)**

By December 1916 the failure of the Russian army caused major concern. At a meeting of generals some comments were:

30 December 1916 Conference of the Commanders-in-Chief

General Ruzski (Northern Front) Riga and Dvinsk – the misfortunes of the Northern Front, especially Riga. These two places are hot beds of propaganda.

Brusilov (Southwest Front) Quite right. When the Seventh Siberian Corps came from the Riga district it was completely under the influence of propaganda. The soldiers refused to fight. There were cases of mutiny. One officer was killed. **(W)**

In February 1917 an army report gave some reasons why the soldiers might rebel:

Among these are the long stay in the trenches . . . alarming news from home about the high cost of living and the decline in the village economy, the misbehaviour of wives at home, and live talks about peace. **(X)**

Factor 8 The Duma and the Zemstvos (local councils)

'Again that fat-bellied Rodzianko has written a lot of nonsense which I won't even bother to answer' wrote Tsar Nicholas on the eve of the March 1917 revolution. Rodzianko was president of the Duma. In August 1914 the Duma gave full support to the Tsar's government – support which the Tsar had lost by 1917. The Tsar refused to accept the advice of the Duma. The Duma warned him about the dangers arising from him being in command of the army, the hatred of the Empress and Rasputin, despair at the inefficient and corrupt government and the shortage of food at St Petersburg. Rodzianko was the link between the Duma and Nicholas. **Y** comes from his memoirs.

20 January 1917 A meeting with the Tsar . . . Russia, as one, demands a change in Government . . . It is vital to work in agreement with the Duma and Zemstvos in order to organise the rear and conquer the enemy. To our great shame in these war times, everything is in disorder. People believe that you have sacked all ministers who had the backing of the Duma and Zemstvos, and put in their place people we cannot trust . . . **(Y)**

Rodzianko had backed a plan for the government to use the Zemstvos to help with the war effort. He got little support from the Tsar. By March 1917 the Tsar had lost the support of the Russians who had backed the

war in 1914. Rodzianko told the Tsar that he had 'pleaded with him not to take the supreme command and that now . . . all the blame fell upon him.' The Tsar was in danger, for it seemed he might 'force your subjects to choose between you and the good of the country.'

On 7 March a food riot began in St Petersburg, which led quickly to the fall of the Tsar's regime, as the following section shows.

??????????????????

1 What thoughts might the soldiers in **F** have about the Tsar and his war role in: September 1914; August 1915; December 1916 (see **D**)?

2 Imagine you are able to interview **a** Alexandra, **b** Rodzianko, in February 1917. What might they tell you about Rasputin? (Character, influence over Alexandra and the Tsar; private life (**J**); role in choosing ministers and advising on military matters (**K**); interference in government; death.)

3 If you could talk to the ghosts of the soldiers in **U**, what might they say about: life in the trenches (treatment, equipment, food . . .); a German artillery attack; the Brusilov offensive and attacking the German front line; news from home?

4 As if you were a helper of Rodzianko, draw up a plan for him to present to the Tsar advising how he can save his throne in February 1917.

5 *Essay title* Why did the Tsar fall from power in March 1917?

　a Copy each of factors 1–8 on to a separate piece of paper.

　b Match one of the sentences below to each factor, and copy it out.

　1 By 1917 the ruling classes in Russia had stopped backing the Tsar.

　2 The economy could not meet the demands of fighting the war.

　3 The growing inefficiency of the government meant the army could not fight properly, there was corruption, breakdown in transport and food shortages.

　4 The Tsar's role as Commander-in-chief meant he was blamed for the army's defeats.

　5 If the Tsar had cooperated with the Duma and the Zemstvos it would have helped win the war.

　6 Alexandra's running of the government lost Nicholas the support of Russia's ruling classes.

　7 By 1917 army officers and soldiers were ready to revolt against the Tsar.

　8 Rasputin's evil influence was blamed for the failure of the government.

　c Use the information on pages 9–13 and anything else you can find to add to each factor.

　d Put the factors in what you think are their order of importance, and use them as your essay plan.

7 The March Revolution

What does it feel like to live through a revolution? Do you think you would know what was going on, and why, if there were no radio or television?

In March 1917 the people and troops of Petrograd overthrew the Tsar. If, on 12 March you had been a member of a crowd like **A**, what might you have seen, heard, thought, hoped and done? **B** lists the main events of the March Revolution. **C–F** are extracts from four accounts of what happened on 12 March in Petrograd. 12 March was the key day in the revolution. To help understand what **C–F** tell you, look at the map of Petrograd on page 24.

Vasiliev is in charge of the police. At 6.00 am on 12 March his telephone rings. He hears of trouble in the Volynskii regiment:

❛ . . . no-one in Petrograd had then the least idea of the turn which events would take. Through my window I could see unusual activity in the street. Soon army cars rushed by, shots were heard in the distance . . . Then events moved fast. The Volynskii Regiment, which had risen after the murder of Captain Lashkevich, had chased its officers out of the barracks. The mutineers joined the Preorbrazhenskii and Lithuanian Regiments of the Guard, whose barracks were near their own. They had succeeded in taking the Arsenal on Leitny Street. Soldiers were dashing about the streets armed with guns and machine-guns. (Nearly all the troops in Petrograd join the mutiny.) I soon left my home, along with my wife and my friend Gvodev. To tell the truth, I did not know where to go, though I had a passport for abroad under a borrowed name. ❜ **(C)**

Maurice Paleologue is the French Ambassador. By 11.00 the revolution is in full swing.

❛ At one corner of Leitny Street, soldiers were helping workers to put up a barricade. Flames shot up from the Law Courts. The gates of the Arsenal burst open with a crash. Suddenly, the crack of machine-gun fire split the air. It was the troops who had just got into place near the Nevsky Prospect . . . The Law Courts had become nothing but a huge furnace, the Arsenal on Leitny Street, the Ministry of the Interior, the Military Government Building . . . the headquarters of the secret police and a score of police stations were in flames. The prisons were open and all the prisoners had been freed. ❜ **(D)**

A Demonstrators gather in front of the Winter Palace, 12 March 1917

B Table of events: 8–15 March 1917

March

Thursday 8 International Women's Day – 90 000 people on strike. Street marches and demonstrations against shortage of bread and fuel.

Friday 9 Strikes spread. Many factories closed – 200 000 workers out. Crowds fill the Nevsky Prospect. Cossack soldiers and police in control of the crowds.

Saturday 10 Large number of factories closed. Huge crowds meet at the Nicholas Station. Cossacks help disperse them. 6.00 – troops fire on crowd in the Nevsky Prospect.

Sunday 11 Trains, cabs and trolleys no longer running. Crowds carry red banners for first time, 'Down with the German woman! Down with the war!' Some companies of troops refuse to fire into the crowds. Extent of unrest leads cabinet to offer its resignation to Nicholas, with a request that he forms a government the Duma can accept. Nicholas refuses, orders army commander of Petrograd to crush the marchers. The Cabinet meets late at night. A sergeant of the Volinskii regiment murders an officer. The regiment mutinies and its officers flee. Other regiments join.

Monday 12 Police and troops join the crowds. The government loses control over Petrograd. By evening the city is in the hands of the mob. They surround and enter the Duma, whose members are arguing about what to do. The crowd wants the Duma to replace the Tsar.

Tuesday 13 Duma sets up a committee to take over the government's powers. In the same building a Soviet of workers and soldiers is formed – the Petrograd Soviet. The Soviet issues *Order No 1* which aims to give it control over troops.

Wednesday 14 The Tsar fails to get to Petrograd on his train. All troops in city loyal to either Duma or the Soviet. Another Soviet formed in Moscow.

Thursday 15 Tsar abdicates. Duma, with support of Petrograd Soviet, forms Provisional Government. Kerensky, key member in Soviet, becomes Minister of Justice in the Provisional Government.

Louis de Robien is a French diplomat. He is with Maurice Paleologue when they visit Leitny Street:

❛. . . *which is filled with numbers of soldiers swarming about in total chaos. Several motor lorries also filled with soldiers, plough their way through the crowd, and we are struck by the small red flags which they carry . . . At this moment, there is a big movement near the bridge, where it would seem that a charge is being made. But, it is impossible to make head or tail of the shambolic ebb and flow of all these panic-stricken people running in every direction. The soldiers we ask know nothing. Clearly, their only interest is in running away. One gets a feeling of total chaos. We return to the embassy, where news has come in over the telephone . . . Serious mutiny has broken out among the troops. All the men we saw belong to regiments sent to restore order, who, after* firing *a few volleys, made common cause with* (joined) *the rebels. All the units sent to fight the mutiny are defecting, one after the other.* ❜ (E)

P Sorokin, a writer, is at home in Old Petersburg on the 12th. The telephone keeps ringing, with news:

❛*"Crowds on the Nevskii Street are bigger than ever today." "Workmen of the Putilovskii factory and of the Vyborg side have gone out into the streets." "Heavy firing is heard from different sides of the town." "They say the Duma has dissolved."*❜

With a friend, Sorokin tries to cross the river by the Troitsky Bridge. Police stop them, so they walk across the ice.

❛. . . *as we turned into Leitny Street the crowd grew larger and much louder grew the sound of the guns. The frantic effort of the police to scatter the crowd had no effect at all. "Ah, Scum! Your end is coming!" howled the mob. From where we stood we could see the red glow of a fire near the Nikolaevskii Station . . . "What is burning?" "The police station . . . We are going to destroy all Government offices, burn, smash, kill all police, all tyrants . . ." With great care we went forward along Leitny Street, and came upon fresh bloodstains and saw two dead bodies on the pavement. Before our horrified eyes a man, trying to cross the street, fell mortally wounded by a flying bullet.*❜ (F)

??????????????

1 **a** Who might be in crowd **A**?
  b Why might Vasiliev need a false passport (**C**)?
  c What happened to the police stations (**D**)?
  d Why were red flags on the lorries (**E**)?
  e How might the two people have died (**F**)?

2 Split up into groups of up to five. Each person take the role of one of the following:
  A Volynskii soldier
  A French diplomat
  A government official going to work in the Law Courts
  A student at the University
  A Putilov factory worker from the Vyborg district
It is 12.00 on 12 March. You all meet in Leitny Street. Tell each other what you know about what is going on; the things you have seen; what has happened to you; your thoughts about the Tsar, the war, the Duma, the government, food shortages and prices.

2 Take one piece of evidence, **A**, **C–F**. How would you check the information which it contains? (Think about: who produced it; why; facts you can check it against; what other sources tell you; internal evidence.)

8 The Provisional Government

The Duma committee talked through the night of 12 March about forming a new government. Crowds broke into the Tauride Palace where they met. Panic set in among committee members:

❝Kerensky then looked at us, and threw the package on the table. "Our secret treaties with the Allies . . . hide them," and disappeared . . . What to do with the secret treaties . . . There was no cupboard, not even a drawer in the table. Some one had an idea, "Throw them under the table: no one will see them."❞ **(A)**

When the crowd left, the Duma members and the Soviet had to decide how they were going to rule Russia. Russia was still at war with Germany, bread was scarce, the government was in chaos, soldiers and sailors were mutinying against their officers. At Kronstadt, Petrograd's naval base, the sailors murdered many of their officers:

❝ . . . before being killed they were slashed and soaked in icy water or petrol. Admiral Wirren was burnt to death in a barrel near the Makharov monument, and his 18-year-old daughter was raped before his eyes and then had her throat cut.❞ **(B)**   (Louis de Robien, diary entry, 17 March 1917)

C lists some of the plans the Soviet and Duma talked about before forming a government. The Duma formed a Provisional Government on 16 March. They decided to follow plans *a, c, e, h, k, n,* and *o–t* (see C). The most crucial decision was on plan *a*: the government decided to fight on against the Germans in support of Russia's allies, Britain and France.

The Duma had the backing of the Soviet. Kerensky, vice-president of the Soviet, became Minister of Justice. The sharing of power between the Duma and the Soviet was called *dual government*. But many Soviet members were against the Provisional Government's plans to go on fighting the war. On 18 May a new Provisional Government was formed. The Soviet now had six members, with Kerensky as Minister of War.

Kerensky faced major problems. Among them were the demands of marchers like those in **D**. **E** describes such a demonstration:

❝I ran into an enormous crowd coming from Nevsky Street. It was a women's demonstration. I walked along the endless procession . . . but I could not reach the head of it which had turned to the right towards the Duma. There were several thousand women arm-in-arm, marching ten to a row, singing

C Plans discussed by the Provisional Government

The war
a The government should back Russia's treaties with its allies, and go on fighting
b It should try and gain peace with Germany on the basis of a return to pre-war boundaries and no payment of money to Germany

The Soviet
c The Soviet should back the Duma
d The Soviet should have nothing to do with a government which is against the interests of the workers

Land
e Land should stay in the hands of those who own it
f It should be split up among the peasants

Food
g The government should take control over all supplies and transport of grain
h It should appeal for the backing of those who own and sell grain – asking them to send what is needed to the towns and the army

The Petrograd Garrison
i It should be treated like all other armed forces
j It should have the right to stay in Petrograd and not lose its arms

The Police
k A new police force should be formed under government control
l A people's militia should be formed, with elected officers, under the control of local elected bodies

The Army
m The army should have its own elected councils to choose officers and run its affairs
n Normal military discipline should be used when soldiers were on duty

Points of agreement
o Freedom of speech and the press
p Freedom to form labour unions and to strike
q Amnesty (pardon) for all political and religious prisoners and offenders
r No religious, class or racial discrimination
s Elections to be held on universal, equal, direct and secret voting right – *suffrage*
t Elections to be held for a Constituent Assembly to decide the form of government and to draw up a constitution for the country.

D Marchers in support of women's rights, Petrograd

revolutionary songs . . . They want the vote for women, more money for the families of those at the Front, but above all the end of the war and the return of the soldiers. A big banner showed the picture of a soldier leaving for the Front, with his wife and children trying to hold him back. ❭ (**E**)

Another problem for Kerensky was the return of Lenin, leader of the Bolsheviks, in April. The Bolsheviks had major support in the Soviet. The German government had helped Lenin to get back from Switzerland in a 'sealed train'. They hoped he would spread unrest in Russia. Can you think why?

At once Lenin announced his *April theses* (**F**) – plans for peace, government takeover of banks and factories and the use of elected soviets to rule Russia.

F Lenin's April Theses

> **The April Theses**
> **1** No support for the Provisional Government
> **2** Immediate end to the war
> **3** A republic of peasants' and workers' Soviets to be set up
> **4** The Soviets to control all economic life – industry, farming, transport, trade
> **5** Nationalisation of banks
> **6** Nationalisation of land
> **7** Abolition of army, police and civil service
> **8** Elected officials working for the Soviets to replace the army, police and civil service
> **9** International body to be set up to spread the revolution world-wide
> **10** Party to win workers and peasants to its views by argument and debate

??????????????

1 Describe scene **D**. What were the women in the crowd hoping to gain (**E**)?

2 For each of the points in the April theses (**F**) say how the following might react on a scale of *a* strongly for *b* for *c* uncertain *d* against *e* strongly against.
- A Menshevik factory worker who is backing Kerensky
- A Petrograd factory owner making shells for the army
- A rich peasant or kulak who farms his own land

3 As if you were members of either the Duma or the Soviet on 15 March, argue about the points you would support under each of the headings in list **C**. Discuss the points in pairs, small groups or as a whole class. (You can choose any one of the headings as an area to research into, to back up your argument.)

9 Kerensky and the July Days

A Alexander Kerensky

As War Minister, in May and June 1917, Kerensky (**A**) prepared the Russian army for an attack on the Austrians in Galicia. Kerensky felt that success in war would gain the Provisional Government the support it needed. **B** and **C** are the views of two diplomats on Kerensky, in mid-1917. **B** comes from Bruce Lockhart, who knew Kerensky well and became a close friend:

❝He was an honest, if not a great man. Sincere, in spite of his oratorical talents (skill as a speaker), *and, for a man who for four months was worshipped as a god, comparatively modest. From the start he was fighting a hopeless battle, trying to drive back into the trenches a nation which had already finished with the war. Caught between the cross-fire of the Bolshevik Left, which was screaming peace at every street-corner and in every trench, and of the Right and of the Allies who were demanding the restoration of discipline by Tsarist methods, he had no chance.* (In a speech in Moscow, Kerensky explained that anything worth having had to be suffered for. The Tsarist regime had left major problems . . .) *. . . disorganised transport, lack of bread, lack of fuel . . . He had just returned from the trenches. He had seen men who had been living for months on end with mud and water up to their knees. Lice crawled over them. For days they had had nothing but a crust of black bread to eat. They were without the proper arms to defend themselves. They had not seen their women-folk for months. Yet they made no complaint. They had promised to do their duty to the end. It was only in Petrograd and Moscow that he heard grumbling. And from whom? From the rich, from those who came here today to listen to him in comfort . . . Were they to bring Russia down in ruins, to be guilty of the most disgraceful betrayal in history, while the poor and humble, who had every reason to complain, were still holding out?❞* (**B**)

C comes from the diary of another diplomat in Petrograd, the Frenchman Louis de Robien:

❝Tuesday, 31 July I met Kerensky again today, in his khaki uniform (he still does not dare dress like a Cossack) installed like the Emperor in the Imperial Rolls-Royce . . . I don't call these people revolutionaries, but just "You clear out and make room for me" people. I much prefer Lenin to these "just-look-at-me" men — at least he is an honest and sincere man . . . Besides (Kerensky) is in reality nothing but an inspired fanatic, a nutcase, and a madman. He acts through intuition and personal ambition, without reasoning and without weighing up his actions. In spite of his undoubted intelligence, his forcefulness and above all his eloquence with which he knows how to lead the mob. All of which show how dangerous he is.❞ (**C**)

D Timechart: May – July 1917

7–12 May	Bolshevik Party Congress in Petrograd, 150 delegates. Nine man central committee under Lenin. 80 000 Bolshevik party members – party three times larger than in March. Policy: all power to the Soviets; end of war, peace without annexations (loss of land) or indemnity (payments); land to the peasants; workers to control factories. Growth of Bolshevik support.
18 May	Coalition government formed. Kerensky Minister of War – prepares Russian army for major summer offensive against the Germans.
16 June	All-Russian Congress of Soviets (see **E**). Bolsheviks play a big role.
22 June	In local elections Bolsheviks gain control over the workers' quarter of Petrograd – the *Vyborg* district.
29 June	Kerensky orders start of the summer offensive – an attack on Galicia.
1 July	Huge demonstrations in Petrograd show massive support for the Bolsheviks and opposition to the war. Outbreak of strikes in Petrograd.
15 July	Four members of cabinet resign after Ukraine given Home Rule. Political crisis.
17 July	Bolshevik crowds with armed soldiers and sailors take to the streets. Bolshevik leaders against any attempt to seize power.
18 July	Government troops close down Bolshevik newspaper, *Pravda* (Truth).
19 July	Government seizes Bolshevik headquarters. Bolshevik leaders go into hiding.
21 July	Kerensky becomes Prime Minister. Failure of the summer offensive. Rout of Russian armies.

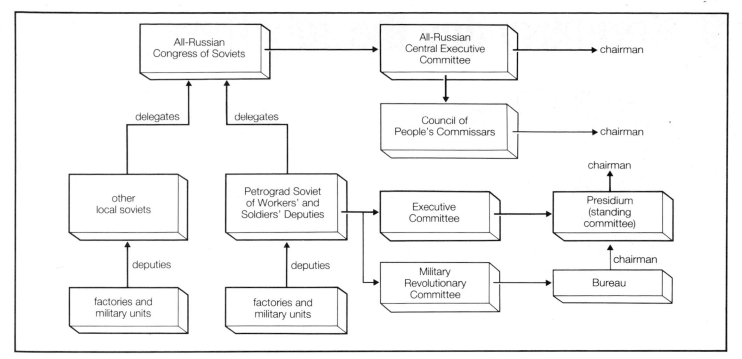

E The system of Soviets, 1917. In each city, town, army or naval garrison the workers, or soldiers and sailors, would elect delegates to their local Soviet. Each Soviet would have its own committee to run local affairs and act in the electorate's interests. Each Soviet sent a delegate to the June meeting of the All-Russia Congress of Soviets

While Kerensky got ready to mount the summer offensive against the Austrians and Germans, Lenin built up the power of the Bolsheviks (see **D**). With the backing of Trotsky and other Mensheviks, Lenin organised the Bolsheviks so that they would be able to seize power when they were ready. Trotsky had close links with the sailors of Kronstadt and the soldiers of the Petrograd garrison. Their support would be vital.

By mid-July the Bolsheviks were increasing their support in the Soviets in most of Russia's towns. But the Social Revolutionaries still had far more backing than the Bolsheviks. A government crisis broke out (see **F**). Bolsheviks in Petrograd feared a new government might arrest them and close down the party. So, against the wishes of Lenin and the other leaders, the Bolshevik supporters took to the streets. As they had feared, the government used the crisis of the July Days to arrest Bolshevik leaders and close down the party. Louis de Robien described what happened in Petrograd:

❝*Leitny Street . . . lorries full of armed men and machine-guns drive through the middle of the crowds of troops, most of whom have rifles. Workmen and soldiers. A lot of sailors . . .* (The government tries to get the Soviet to restore order. Fighting breaks out in Leitny Street.)
17 July 1917 *I had hardly got in when a loud burst of firing made me run to the window. The crowd was fleeing madly, riderless horses were galloping among running soldiers who were throwing away their arms.* (18 July – the government regains control of Petrograd.)
19 July *The government announced yesterday evening that it is going to have Lenin and the ringleaders arrested and accused of treason. It claims to have proof that they received money from Germany.* ❞ (**F**)

??????????????

1 Think of six words to describe the character of Kerensky as shown in **A**. Use these words, **B** and **C**, to write a paragraph about Kerensky.

2 a Make notes on the views of Kerensky given in **B** and **C**.
  b Discuss, in pairs or groups, points on which the diplomats agree or disagree, and why.
  c What evidence can you find to support their different viewpoints?

3 What problems do sources **B**, **C**, **D** and **F** pose as historical evidence?

4 You arrive at school. The teachers have decided to set up a Soviet of pupils to run it. As a class, you have to decide:
  • how the Soviet should be run, membership etc.
  • plans you want to carry out
  • what steps you will take if teachers ignore these plans or are told not to carry them out

10 The Kornilov Revolt

A Timechart: the Kornilov Revolt

21 August	Lenin flees, in disguise, into hiding in Finland.
25 August	Bolshevik party meeting. Trotsky and supporters now official members of Bolshevik party.
6 September	Kornilov (army commander) begins to move troops towards Petrograd. Aims to destroy the Soviet, and reorganise the Provisional Government. Kornilov thinks he has Kerensky's backing.
9 September	Kerensky dismisses Kornilov. Kornilov tries to move troops to Petrograd. Railway workers refuse to let trains pass. Kornilov's troops persuaded not to fight against the Soviet. Kornilov's rising grinds to a halt. Petrograd Soviet organises to fight Kornilov. 'Committee for the Struggle with the Counterrevolution' set up. Bolsheviks in the majority. Bolshevik leaders released from jail to fight Kornilov.
12 September	End of Kornilov revolt. Bolsheviks in majority in Petrograd Soviet. Lenin pushes plan of 'all power to the Soviets'. Trotsky organises Red Guards in factories with rifles and machine guns – some 25 000 strong under Bolshevik Military Organisation.

B General Kornilov

D Red Guards outside the Moscow telephone exchange, seized in October 1917

The July Days were a disaster for Lenin and the Bolsheviks. In August Lenin fled to Finland, fearing for his life. Yet within two months Lenin was to head a Bolshevik Revolution which seized power from Kerensky's government. Why? How? **A** lists the main events of the rising of September 1917. The Kornilov affair was a key factor. Kornilov (**B**), Commander-in-chief of the army, had had talks with Kerensky about how to strengthen both army and government to help win the war. By 6 September although he was at the front, Kornilov thought he had the support of Kerensky for his plan to reform the government together with Kornilov as dictator. But, on 9 September Kerensky sacked Kornilov having learnt that Kornilov meant to seize power.

Kornilov had the backing of the army's generals and officers, and he made an appeal to all Russians on 11 September:

❛ . . . the Provisional Government, under the pressure of the Bolshevik majority in the Soviets, is acting in total harmony with the German General Staff. At the same time, with the expected landing of the enemy troops near Riga, the government is killing the army and killing the country . . . I call upon all Russians to save their dying land. All in whose breast a Russian heart beats, all who believe in God, in the Church, pray to Him for the greatest miracle – the saving of our native land . . . I, general Kornilov, son of a Cossack peasant . . . ❜
(**C**)

To defeat Kornilov, Kerensky was forced to release the Bolsheviks' leaders from jail and rely on their Red Guards (**D**) and the Petrograd Soviet. The Kornilov affair meant Kerensky had lost army support. He could not stop the Bolsheviks from building up their strength.

11 Town and Country, October 1917

The failure of Kornilov meant the Bolsheviks could build up their support in the countryside, the towns and the factories (see **A**, **B** and **C**).

The countryside

By mid-1917 the peasants were starting to take over the land from their landlords. An eyewitness tells us:

Each year the peasants rented their land from the landlord . . . This year they went to him as usual and he asked the usual rent. The peasants refused to pay it and went home. There they called a meeting and decided to take the land without paying. They put the ploughs and harrows on their carts and started for the field. When they arrived they got into a row about splitting up the land . . . It ended in another fight in which three were killed and five badly wounded. One of the peasants, whose son was killed, shook his fist and shouted: "I will make you pay for my son." Three days later one of the village houses caught fire. **(A)**

Town Life

John Reed, an American journalist who backed the Bolsheviks, lived in St Petersburg in 1917. In 1919 he described life there in his book *Ten Days that Shook the World:*

September and October are the worst months of the Russian year – especially the Petrograd year. Under dull grey skies, in the shortening days, the rain fell drenching, incessant. The mud underfoot was deep, slippery and clinging, tracked everywhere by heavy boots, and worse than usual because of the complete breakdown of the Municipal administration. At night, for motives of economy as well as fear of Zeppelins (airships used on bombing raids), the streetlights were few and far between; in private dwellings and apartment houses the electricity was turned on from six o'clock until midnight, with candles 40 cents apiece and little kerosene to be had. It was dark from three in the afternoon to ten in the morning. Robberies and housebreaking increased. In apartment houses the men took turns at all-night guard duty, armed with loaded rifles. This was under the Provisional Government.

Week by week food became scarcer. The daily allowance of bread fell from a pound and a half to a pound, then three quarters, half, and a quarter-pound. Towards the end there was a week without any bread at all. Sugar, one was entitled to at the rate of two pounds a month – if one could get it at all, which was seldom. A bar of chocolate or a pound of tasteless candy cost anywhere from seven to ten roubles – at least a dollar. There was milk for about half the babies in the city; most hotels and private houses never saw it for months . . .

For milk and bread and sugar and tobacco one had to stand and queue long hours in the chill rain. Coming home from an all-night meeting I have seen the kvost (tail) beginning to form before dawn, mostly women, some with babies in their arms . . . **(B)**

The factories

Day after day the Bolshevik orators (speakers) toured the barracks and factories . . . One Sunday we went . . . to a government arms factory on Schlusselburg Street. The meeting took place between the gaunt brick walls of a huge unfinished building, 10 000 black-clothed men and women packed around a platform draped in red, people heaped on piles of wood and bricks . . . A slight, student-like figure . . . was telling us why the power must be taken by the Soviets. Nothing else could guarantee the Revolution against its enemies . . . A soldier from the Rumanian Front, thin, tragical and fierce, cried, "Comrades! We are starving at the Front, we are stiff with cold. We are dying for no reason . . . **(C)**

??????????????????

1 Complete the following sentences
  a on 25 August Trotsky . . .
  b Kornilov planned . . .
  c Kerensky dismissed . . .
  d After the Kornilov revolt, the Bolsheviks . . .

2 Give five reasons why Kornilov was defeated. In pairs, put them in your order of importance. Then as a class work out what you think the most important reasons were. Which of these factors do you think strengthened the Bolsheviks? Why?

3 Imagine you are at a meeting of the poor peasants in **A** after the events described. Act out, or discuss, what you are going to do and what will happen next.

4 Copy out these Bolshevik slogans: 'Peace, Bread, Land,' 'All power to the Soviets'. Under each one, write down any evidence in **A**, **B** or **C** that suggests the Bolsheviks might get support from people or groups mentioned in the extracts.

12 The Bolsheviks Prepare

During September and October 1917 the Bolsheviks won control over the Soviets of Russia's towns and cities (see **A**). When the Pre-Parliament (the nationally-elected body which met to draw up the constitution) met on 20 October, rumours spread that the Bolsheviks were plotting to seize power. Louis de Robien noted:

❛The quarrel between the Bolsheviks and the government has become much worse since the first session of the Pre-Parliament . . . The Bolsheviks . . . announced the breaking off of all ties with the government, and threatened to achieve their purpose by any means they think proper. It is a real declaration of war.❜ (**B**)

The following sections look at some of the reasons why, in November 1917, the Bolsheviks were ready to seize power. Lenin's role was central.

Lenin's role

After the Kornilov revolt Lenin pressed hard for a Bolshevik-led revolution (**C**). He feared that if the Bolsheviks waited for a meeting of all of Russia's Soviets, the Social Revolutionaries and Mensheviks would outvote them. On 28 September Lenin wrote from hiding in Finland:

❛Without losing a single moment . . . arrest the general staff and the government . . . we must mobilise the armed workers . . . occupy at once the telegraph and telephone stations . . .❜ (**D**)

A Table of events: the Bolshevik Revolution

19 September	Bolshevik majority in Moscow Soviet.
8 October	Kerensky forms new coalition government, and continues war policy. Bolsheviks in majority in Petrograd Soviet.
17 October	Kerensky government plans to leave Petrograd in face of German advance. This news causes uproar among Petrograd Soviet members.
20 October	Pre-Parliament of all Russian political parties meets in Petrograd to plan the future of the country's politicial system. Lenin returns from exile in Finland.
23 October	Bolsheviks walk out of Pre-Parliament's first session. Bolshevik Party Central Committee secretly decides to mount a rising against the government.
24 October	Meeting of Congress of northern Russian Soviets. Trotsky announces time has come for the Soviets to seize power.
25 October	Executive Committee of Petrograd Soviet sets up Military Revolutionary Committee to organise the revolution.

Most of the Bolshevik leaders in Petrograd were against Lenin's plan to seize power. In October growing fears changed the Bolshevik leaders' minds. It seemed that Kerensky would remove the government from Petrograd and even surrender it to the Germans. News also spread of Kerensky's plans to arrest the Bolshevik leaders. On 23 October Lenin won over the Bolshevik leaders to his side.

During the evening of 5 November Lenin made his way disguised to the headquarters of the MRC (Military Revolutionary Committee). The MRC's plans were in danger from Kerensky's troops. Lenin took charge of the MRC and gave the orders which helped the Bolsheviks gain power.

The organisation of the Bolshevik Party

The Central Committee of the Bolshevik Party built up a strong organisation (**E**). From its Petrograd headquarters it founded party committees throughout Russia and within the army. Stalin ran the party newspaper *Pravda* (Truth), which spread Bolshevik propaganda and news. Trotsky was in charge of the party's Red Guard – a force of armed workers and soldiers.

❛At Kronstadt a Red Guard has been set up. All the workmen of the fortress have been supplied with arms. Daily they are being drilled in the use of rifles. Today there was a meeting at Moscow of the Soviet to discuss the question of a Red Guard. It was decided to arm the workers as soon as possible.❜
(**F**)   (Newspaper report, 28 September)

Each factory set up its own Red Guard. By mid-October they were getting rifles from the government arms factory at Sestroretsk on the Gulf of Finland. For the November revolution Trotsky could call for help on some 25 000 armed Red Guards.

C Lenin speaking to the crowds in Red Square, Moscow

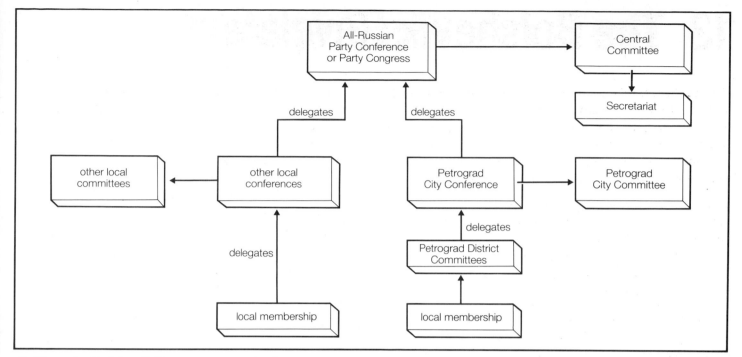

E How the Bolshevik Party was organised

Bolshevik plans and propaganda

By mid-October the ideas of Lenin and the Bolsheviks had spread through the factories, the army and the navy. **G** shows the main ideas in the 'Bolshevik declaration' of 16 October.

The Bolshevik Party was also in charge of the Petrograd Soviet. Bolsheviks won a majority of members in elections to the Soviet in September. Trotsky was elected Soviet Chairman on 12 September. The Bolsheviks ran the Soviet's Military Revolutionary Committee, and used it to organise the revolution.

G The Bolshevik Declaration of 16 October

1 Private property to be taken from the landowners without payment. Land to be handed over to peasant committees. Poorest peasants to be given tools.
2 Workers to have control over industry and trade. *Nationalisation* (government takeover) of main industries – oil, coal, iron and steel. Seizing of war profits.
3 Offer of peace to all powers at once.
4 Promise of freedom to nationalities of Russia. (There were many races in Russia, such as the Poles and Latvians. They might want to set up their own countries.) End of repression of Finland and the Ukraine.
5 Troops to elect their own officials. Complete freedom of agitation in the army. (Freedom to make speeches, spread ideas and distribute newspapers, pamphlets and books.) Workers to be armed. Red Guard to be set up.
8 Eight-hour working day and introduction of social insurance.

(These points were summed up in the slogans, 'Peace, Bread and Land' and 'All Power to the Soviets'.)

??????????????????

1 Copy and fill in the chart below to show which of the plans listed in **G** would be most likely to appeal to the following people: (One has been done for you)

	a great deal	a little	not at all
A peasant			
A Ukrainian officer			
A Petrograd factory worker	2		
A Finnish soldier			
A Petrograd shop owner			
A member of the Petrograd garrison			

2 Imagine it is October 1917. Your form are members of a school in Petrograd. A Bolshevik agitator has come to your school and wants your class to set up a Bolshevik 'cell'. How would you go about it? (Discuss: membership; leaders; party policy; delegates to party conference; feelings for or against revolution – other plans.)

3 What points might the Bolshevik leaders have made *against* Lenin's plans in October for a revolution? (*Clues* July Days/The Army/Kerensky/Congress of all Russia's Soviets/German spy scare/Mensheviks and Social Revolutionaries.)

13 The Bolshevik Revolution

For the Bolsheviks to succeed they had to be sure that Kerensky could not get the army to crush a Bolshevik rising. The Bolsheviks would need the backing of the army's Petrograd garrison. By October 1917 the officers were still in command of the army. It had been able in the Brusilov offensive to defeat the Austrians. Russia's factories and farms produced enough food, guns, ammunition, clothes and equipment to enable the army to fight on. At the front line and in the barracks the Bolsheviks tried to win over the soldiers to their ideas. In Petrograd, John Reed visited the building where the Circus was usually held. The hall:

❝*was packed from the ring up the steep sweep of grimy benches to the very roof – soldiers, sailors, workmen, women, all listening as if their lives depended upon it. A soldier was speaking – from the 548th Division, wherever and whatever that was: "Comrades", he cried . . . "tell me what I am fighting for. Is it Constantinople or is it free Russia? Is it the Democracy or is it the Capitalist plunderers? If you can prove to me that I am defending the Revolution then I'll go out and fight without capital punishment to force me. When the land belongs to the peasants, and the factories to the workers, and the power to the Soviets, then we'll have something to fight for, and we'll fight for it!" In the barracks, the factories, on the street corners, endless soldier speakers all clamour for an end to the war.*❞ (A)

Army Intelligence reports for October stated:

❝*Northern Front The influence of Bolshevik ideas is spreading rapidly. To this must be added a general tiredness, bad temper and a wish for peace at any price . . .*

Western Front . . . refusals to carry out orders, threats to the officers and attempts to be friendly with the Germans. Everywhere one hears voices calling for an immediate peace, because, they say, no one will stay in the trenches during the winter . . .❞ (B)

On 3 November the Military Revolutionary Committee sent Bolshevik agents (*commissars*) to win over the men of the Petrograd garrison to support the Bolshevik rising. When the garrison commanders refused to back the Bolsheviks, the MRC under Trotsky issued a printed statement that the troops of the garrison were to take their orders from the MRC and not from their officers.

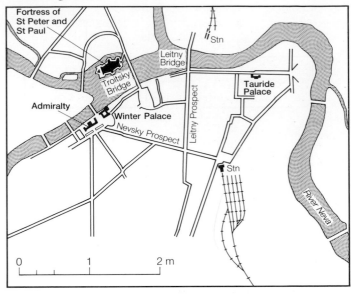

C Petrograd

D Kerensky's plans

1 Call in the army commanders with their troops from the front line, to put down Bolsheviks. Kerensky has just visited army headquarters.
2 Withdraw the government to Moscow, leaving Petrograd in the hands of the Germans.
3 Make peace with Austria–Hungary, and agree to a ceasefire with the Germans.
4 Move 1000 army officers into Petrograd in secret so that they command troops in a move against the Bolsheviks.
5 Use the Petrograd garrison against the Bolsheviks.
6 Post troops in favour of the Bolsheviks from Petrograd to the front line.
7 Seize and destroy the Bolshevik printing presses and headquarters.
8 Arrest the Bolshevik leaders and shoot them.
9 Form a coalition with all other parties and groups to crush the Bolsheviks.

Rumours of plots and counterplots swept through Petrograd (C) in early November. The Bolsheviks in the Soviet and on the MRC were afraid that Kerensky might carry out some of the plans in D.

In turn, Kerensky knew that the Bolsheviks were getting ready to overthrow the Provisional Government. On 5 November Kerensky began his moves against the Bolsheviks. These led to the events outlined in E.

23 October	Lenin persuades the Bolshevik central committee to prepare for revolution. It is planned to begin on 6/7 November – at the same time as a meeting of the All-Russian Congress of Soviets.
3 November	MRC gains control of the Petrograd garrison.
5 November	Kerensky begins to act against the Bolsheviks by closing down newspaper offices. Trotsky announces the start of hostilities.
6 November	Trotsky gains support of troops in the Peter and Paul fortress. During the night Bolsheviks and Red Guards capture the Telephone Exchange, power stations, rail stations, banks and main bridges in Petrograd.
7 November	Kerensky leaves the city unopposed, hoping to gain support from troops elsewhere. Bolsheviks continue to take over Petrograd. By mid-afternoon only the Winter Palace remains – where the Provisional Government is sitting. 9.40 pm The cruiser *Aurora*, moored in the River Neva, fires a shell in the direction of the Winter Palace – the signal for the Red Guards to attack (**F**). They meet little opposition, and the Provisional Government surrenders without a struggle.
8 November	Around 1.00 am news of the revolution reaches the All-Russian Congress. Lenin is at the meeting, in disguise. He stands and announces: 'Comrades, the workers' and peasants' revolution . . . has come to pass . . . we shall have a Soviet Government, without the participation of a bourgeoisie of any kind. The oppressed masses will themselves form a government.'
8–15 November	Revolutions take place in other Russian cities, including Moscow.

E Table of events: November 1917

F Storming the Winter Palace

?????????????????

1 What did the soldier in **A** mean by: Constantinople; free Russia; Democracy; capitalist plunderers; power to the Soviets?

2 The statements below are in the wrong order. Match them up with the dates in the order the events took place:

3 Nov Bolsheviks drive Kerensky out of Petrograd
5 Nov After a week's struggle Bolsheviks win control of Moscow
6 Nov MRC gains support of Petrograd garrison
7 Nov Kerensky's supporters smash Bolshevik printing presses
15 Nov Bolsheviks storm Winter Palace

Now use these statements to write a short account of events during the Bolshevik Revolution of 1917.

3 Split into pairs (or two groups): Kerensky's advisers v. members of the MRC. Look at list **D** and map **C**.

Kerensky's advisers:

Which of the plans in **D** will you follow?
How should you carry them out?
Work out in detail how to protect key government positions and buildings.

Bolshevik leaders:

How will you stop Kerensky carrying out each of the plans in **D**?
Which buildings and key points will you seize, and in what order?
Now compare your ideas with those of the other group. Would Kerensky have been able to carry out his plans and defeat the Bolsheviks? Or would the Revolution have succeeded? Compare your ideas with what actually happened in November 1917.

14 The Civil War

In 1917 Lenin and the Bolsheviks (now known as the Communists or *Reds*) had seized control over Petrograd and Moscow quite easily. But could they hang on to power? They controlled only part of Russia (see map **A**). Many groups opposed them. The Mensheviks, Social Revolutionaries and supporters of the Tsar said they had no right to rule. These opponents came to be known as the *Whites*. Many Whites hated the Reds because they seized the land, property and factories of the well-off and because they attacked religious beliefs. By the end of 1918 there was civil war between the Whites and the Reds.

The Allies (Britain, France, the USA and Japan) sent supplies and troops to help the Whites. The Allies were angry because Lenin had made peace with Germany in the Treaty of Brest-Litovsk, in March 1918. The terms were harsh. Russia lost much territory including Finland, Estonia, Latvia, Lithuania and Poland. The Reds refused to repay loans made to the Tsar's government, and had nationalised foreign-owned businesses in Russia without compensation.

A The Civil War

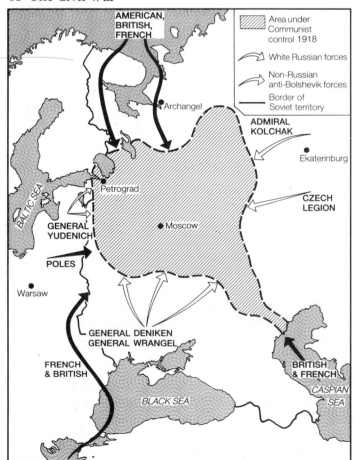

B Trotsky addresses Red Soldiers in Moscow

The job of defeating the Whites fell to Leon Trotsky (**B**) the Commissar for War. His first task was to create an army – a Red Army of workers and peasants. It was not an easy task, as Trotsky explained:

Our best regiments were unstable and unreliable (could not be trusted). *Whole regiments of peasants surrendered without a struggle in the early days.* (**C**)

Trotsky had to use threats and terror against his own men:

Order of the Revolutionary war council, 24 November 1918, No. 65 . . . Every scoundrel who urges anyone to retreat, desert or not obey an order, will be shot. Every soldier who throws away his rifle or sells part of his equipment, will be shot. Houses in which deserters are found will be burnt down. (**D**)

Trotsky directed the war from a special train, which enabled him to race from front to front. On board it had:

* . . . *a printing press, a telegraph station, a radio station, an electric power station, a library, a garage with cars and a bath . . . a squad of hand-picked sharp shooters and machine gunners occupied the trucks.* (**E**)

The Reds also had a new secret police – the *Cheka*. The Cheka shot thousands of people in what became known as the 'Red Terror'. Many people were killed not because of what they had done but because of what they were – kulaks, priests or bourgeoisie. One Cheka leader told his men:

Do not demand incriminating evidence to prove that the prisoner has opposed the Soviet government by force or words. Your first duty is to ask him to which class he belongs, what are his origins, his education, his occupation. These questions should decide the fate of the prisoner. (F)

The most famous victims of the Cheka were the Tsar and his family. No bodies were ever found. But it is almost certain that the Cheka shot the Tsar, his son and possibly his wife and daughters at Ekaterinburg in July 1918.

The Whites behaved no better. They also murdered and tortured opponents and innocent people. In one village a hole was made in the ice and every villager was pushed under. The officers mistreated their men. A British officer, Major Hodges, wrote:

There was corruption and cowardice. White officers swindled the men of their food and clothes. It was revolting to see wounded men dragging their way from station to hospital over dirty streets while white officers rode scornfully by in droshkies (carriages) or motor cars. (G)

Whoever was in control many peasants suffered. Both sides stole food and animals. Some peasants formed *partisan* (resistance) groups to defend themselves.

The first threat to the area controlled by the Reds came from the Czech Legion. These were Czechs who had fought with the Tsar's army against Austria–Hungary, to free Czechs from Austrian rule. The Czech Legion's barracks were in Siberia. The Communists tried to disarm them, so they took control of parts of the Trans-Siberian Railway and joined with Admiral Kolchak and his White troops.

Kolchak led the first of the three main armies which fought the Red Army. He attacked from the east in the spring of 1918, but by the summer of 1919 he was defeated.

Next, from the south, came General Deniken's army, helped by Cossacks and the French. They advanced quickly towards Moscow but as Baron Wrangel, second in command, explained:

We had bitten off far more than we could chew. Our front was too long for the number of men we had, we had no organised bases, and no strongholds in our rear. (H)

By November 1919 Deniken was retreating. He fled, but Wrangel continued to hold out for another year. In the north General Yudenich's army, helped by British tanks, attacked Petrograd. By November they were also defeated. The Allies now went home.

In April 1920 the Poles attacked Russia, hoping to regain land which had once belonged to Poland. The Poles were pushed back but stopped the Red Army at the Battle of the Vistula. Peace was agreed. In the Treaty of Riga in March 1921, Lenin handed over the land Poland claimed.

By 1921 the Civil War had ended. The Communists had won. There were many reasons for their victory. **J** and **K** are evidence of two of these reasons:

A journalist wrote in 1920:

The majority of the (White) officers objected both to fighting and working . . . many officers swindled the men of their food and clothes. (J)

An historian wrote in 1973:

The Bolsheviks held the central region including Moscow and Petrograd. The war tended to be fought along railway routes which centred on Moscow and Petrograd . . . enabling the Reds to shift troops from one front to another at short notice. (K)

L shows some of the other reasons for the Communist success.

L Reasons for Communist success

> **a** The Whites had no single commander, and no single plan. The Whites disliked each other, and would not co-operate.
> **b** The Reds had control of Russia's capital.
> **c** The Reds had internal lines of communication, and could use the railways to switch their troops quickly between fronts, and bring them to where they were needed.
> **d** The foreign Allies of the Whites sent little aid, and withdrew their forces before the war was over.

??????????????????

1 Explain the terms: Whites; Reds; Cheka; Czech Legion.

2 What did the Cheka leader mean in **F** when he said, 'ask him what class he belongs to'?

3 Write a short speech which Trotsky might be making in **B** to encourage his troops. (Include the following words: Whites, peasants, victory, the Tsar, the Allies.)

4 Why did the Whites lose the Civil War? Write an essay answering this question:
   a draw up a list of points using the evidence in this chapter;
   b by each point write down at least two facts or pieces of evidence which support that viewpoint;
   c in groups, or as a class, draw up your essay plan to answer the question;
   d write your own first paragraph to introduce the essay.

15 War Communism, 1918–21

During the Civil War, Lenin had to make sure the Red Army had enough food and weapons. He hoped to do this by strict communist control of industry and food supplies. Lenin's policy was called War Communism. Many orders were passed, such as **A**:

All citizens are subject to compulsory labour . . except persons under 16 or over 50, persons who are disabled by injury or illness, pregnant women for a period of eight weeks before and after confinement. **(A)**

B shows the main measures of War Communism.

B War Communism

1 State control of the means of production, including factories, mines, workshops and railways.
2 Private trading banned.
3 Grain to be requisitioned (seized) from the peasants.
4 State control of banks, payment by goods rather than money.

War Communism was not a success. Many peasants hid their grain. They did not want to sell it to the Communist Government as the money they got in return was nearly worthless. In any case there was little to buy with it. The Government ordered groups of soldiers and workers to take grain by force:

6 August 1918 Grain voluntarily surrendered is to be paid for at a fixed price . . . hidden grain is subject to confiscation. 20 August Every food requisition group is to consist of not less than 75 men and two or three machine guns. **(C)**

Even so, seizing the grain was not easy:

A small company was sent to a village to requisition the bread reserves . . . They were disarmed by the peasants . . . Another company with two machine guns was sent, and they returned without the machine guns. A third company was ordered out . . . the peasants opened fire and killed six . . . A fourth and much better armed force was sent and recaptured the machine guns (but not the bread). **(D)**

Many trains broke down and were not mended. Not enough food reached the towns and there was strict rationing. Workers and soldiers received most food, the middle-class and formerly wealthy people got almost nothing. At times even the workers' ration was below starvation level. Many people could keep themselves alive only if they had something to trade for food on the illegal market – the black market. One girl of ten,

Margot Tracey, whose parents had been arrested, described how she survived with her friend Tousia by using the black market:

We visited nearby black markets in search of food . . . All the time we were on the look out for soldiers who raided these places . . . Money was worthless . . . Peasants exchanged food only for articles of clothing or household goods . . . Once we bartered a precious possession for a sheep's head only to discover on closer examination that it was the head of a dog, and probably an old one at that. We cooked it just the same, wasting precious fuel, but the smell proved so revolting it made us both sick.

The two girls quickly learnt how to use the black market:

Our staple diet when things were grim was potato peelings fried. One evening we found a large, black crow, frozen solid, Tousia plucked it, cutting off its feet and head, and tied it up . . . we now had the most magnificent chicken. **(E)**

They swopped the old crow, made to look like a chicken, for potatoes and fat.

Thousands of workers and their families left the towns and fled to the countryside in search of food. Other workers made things like penknives or cigarette lighters to swop for food. Fuel and raw materials were in short supply. The output of industry fell sharply **(F)**. Inflation went mad. Money was nearly worthless. The cost of a train journey in November 1922 was four million times higher than in June 1917.

By 1921 the Communists had won the Civil War. But that year famine hit Russia. For three years there had been bread shortages and now the harvest failed. The old and sick were first to die. Starving peasants went to the railway stations to wait for food, and died there **(G)**. Some turned to crime, cannibalism and bodysnatching. The peasants in **H** made a living by

F Industrial output in 1913 and 1921 (in tons)

	1913	1921
Coal	29 000 000	8 900 000
Oil	9 200 000	3 800 000
Steel	4 300 000	200 000
Sugar	1 300 000	50 000
Rail freight	132 400 000	39 400 000
Electricity (million KWhs)	2039	520

G Thousands of poor peasants faced starvation

H Traders in human flesh

selling human flesh to the starving. A Russian doctor wrote:

'Sometimes a starving family eats the body of one of its junior members . . . sometimes parents at night take part of a body from the cemetery and feed it to their children.' (J)

Diseases like typhus and cholera killed thousands. Food was sent from other countries but even so about five million people died. It is difficult for us to understand the suffering of these people. Walter Duranty, an American journalist in Russia, visited the famine areas and was shocked:

'The first thing I saw, and smelt, was a refugee camp of about 15 000 peasants, outside the railway station . . . The adults were haggard but far less dreadful than the children with bloated bellies and shrivelled limbs. That came from eating clay and bark and refuse . . . Like cattle in a drought they waited for death. The only movement among them was the stretcher bearers carrying off the dead.

I went to a "children's home", which was more like a "pound" for dogs. Most were past hunger, one child of seven with fingers no thicker than matches refused the chocolate I offered him and just turned his head away. Inside the house children in all stages of different diseases huddled together . . . I went away . . . hating myself for being healthy and well fed.' (K)

??????????????

1 What do you understand by: War Communism; the black market?

2 Study **B**. Explain how each measure (**1–4**) might help Lenin send supplies to the Red Army in the Civil War.

3 Look at **F**.
   a Which two industries suffered the greatest fall in output 1913–21?
   b What reasons can you think of for the decline in industrial output during the Civil War?

4 Imagine you were with Margot Tracey in 1921. Write about: the different ways you might get food; life in a refugee camp; what you would like to say to Lenin to persuade him to end War Communism.

5 a Match each of the sources **A–K** with one of the following types of evidence: journalist's story; personal story; eyewitness account; historian's account; government order; photograph.
   b How reliable do you think each is in helping us see what actually went on in Russia from 1918–22? Give reasons for your answers.

16 The New Economic Policy 1921–28

At the end of 1920, revolts against War Communism began. In Petrograd strikers said:

❝ *A complete change is necessary . . . The workers and peasants need freedom. They don't want to live by the orders of the Bolsheviks, they want to control their own decisions.* ❞ (A)

The most serious revolt was in March 1921 at the naval base of Kronstadt, on an island near Petrograd. The sailors of Kronstadt were angry at the hardships and the increasing violence used by the Communist Party to control the workers and peasants. They wanted to be free of strict rule. They took over Kronstadt and demanded:

❝ *. . . new elections to the Soviets with a secret vote, freedom of speech and press . . . freedom to meet for trade unions and peasant groups . . . freedom for peasants to farm their land.* ❞ (B)

Lenin refused. He believed the Communist Party had to be in complete control if the revolution was to survive. When the sailors and workers refused to surrender, Trotsky ordered the Red Army to attack – by marching across the frozen sea (C). General Takhachevsky, in command of the attack, wrote:

❝ *The sailors fought like wild beasts . . . Each house had to be taken by storm. An entire company fought for an hour to capture one house, it contained two or three men at a machine gun. They seemed half-dead, but they snatched their revolvers and gasped "Too little did we shoot at you scoundrels."* ❞ (D)

When the Red Army won it showed little mercy. A Russian, Alexander Berkman wrote:

C Red Soldiers cross the ice to attack Kronstadt

G 'Nepmen' and customers in Smolensk market, Moscow

❝ *The city ran red with the blood of Kronstadt men, women and children. For several weeks the Petrograd jails were filled with hundreds of Kronstadt prisoners. Every night small groups of them were taken out by the Cheka and disappeared.* ❞ (E)

The Kronstadt revolt, together with the famine, made Lenin realise he must end War Communism. But how was he to persuade the peasants to produce more food for the town workers? His answer was the New Economic Policy (NEP). In March 1921 Lenin announced:

❝ *We are in a condition of such poverty, ruin and exhaustion . . . that everything must be set aside to increase production.* ❞ (F)

The aim was to give Russia a breathing space in which to recover. Lenin ended the seizing of grain by force. He replaced it with a tax, paid in grain, of a fixed percentage of the harvest. Now the peasants knew that any surplus grain they grew could be sold. So they grew more grain. Now the peasants had money, they wanted to buy things. Private trade was allowed again and private traders, or *nepmen* as they were known, re-appeared (G). Walter Duranty, the American journalist, saw how NEP worked:

❝ *One morning I saw a man sitting on the sidewalk selling flour, sugar and rice. By May he had a fair-sized store, to* which peasants brought fresh produce each morning. In July he opened a dry goods section, then added hardware . . . After a year's trading . . . he made $20 000 or $30 000 clear profit, but the point is that his enterprise stimulated peasants to fatten chickens and plant vegetables . . . The same thing was being done all over Russia. In a single year the supply of food and goods jumped from starvation point to something nearly adequate, and prices fell accordingly. *)* **(H)**

Under the NEP businessmen could set up small, privately-owned factories employing up to 20 workers. Forced labour was ended, bonuses were allowed and workers were paid in money rather than goods. In 1925 the kulaks, the wealthier peasants, could hire people to work for them. All this horrified many communists, such as Anna Strong who wrote:

(In my few short trips into Moscow streets during the winter of 1921–22, I had been disturbed by the growing private trade. To me each seems a step of defeat . . . There's a horrible new rich set growing.) **(J)**

Her communist friend argued:

(But it is better than letting men starve. We began with ruin and were forced into civil war, we met blockade and famine. This means we must allow private trade and private work- shops . . . Later, as state industries produce a surplus these will expand and drive out private trade. *)* **(K)**

This friend understood what Lenin was trying to do. Lenin made sure that the State was still in charge of banking, foreign trade and what he called the 'Commanding heights' of industry – coal, iron, steel, oil, electricity and the railways. Lenin explained:

(We are now retreating, going back as it were, but we are doing this so as to retreat first and then run and leap forward more vigorously . . . The workers' regime is in no danger as they firmly hold transport and large scale industry.) **(L)**

The NEP helped rescue Russia from the economic disaster of 1920–21. There was more food, and industry expanded (see **M**). Walter Duranty reported what a difference NEP made to life in Moscow:

(Shops, cafes and restaurants were being opened . . . traffic had increased tenfold. The city was full of peasants selling fruit, vegetables, or transporting building materials.) **(N)**

Other changes also took place. More hospitals and schools were built. The Russian government was re-organised. In 1923 Russia became the Union of Soviet Socialist Republics (USSR) – a union of four republics, each ruled by its own Soviet. In practice, however, the Communist Party leaders – the members of the Politburo in Moscow – took all important decisions.

M Production in key industries 1913–25

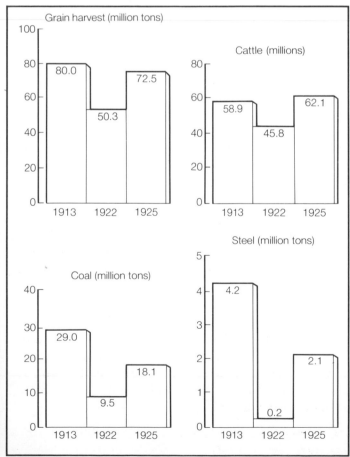

???????????????

① What freedoms did the Kronstadt sailors and workers demand (**A**)? Why?

②a Look at **C**. What can you learn from it about the fighting at Kronstadt?
b How do you think the man in **H** was able to make a profit?
c Do the figures in **M** suggest that agriculture or industry was more successful in recovering production by 1925? Why was one more successful than the other?
d How can we check that sources **C**, **H** and **M** are telling us the truth?

③ How successful was the New Economic Policy? In pairs, discuss ways in which it was a success. Write down your points. Under each point, write the evidence which supports it. Then use these notes as a basis for your essay, beginning 'The New Economic Policy was successful in a number of ways. The first success was . . .'.

17 Stalin's Rise to Power

A Joseph Stalin

The revolution is over. Your teachers have fled. You have to choose someone to run the school. He or she will be a member of your year. Which of the points below do you think are most important? Should the person you want:

1 organise and run one of the school's main sports teams;

2 have lots of ideas about how lessons should be taught, and the subjects you should take;

3 have lots of friends in the year, who are all liked and respected;

4 be able to organise discos, the school magazine, school tuckshop . . . and have friends in all the important jobs. Organise election of self and friends to the school council;

5 plan to spread ideas of pupil control to other schools in the area?

Lenin died in January 1924. Now the nine Bolshevik leaders in the Politburo faced the same kind of problem as you might face. Who should run Russia after Lenin? Two men seemed most likely to become the new ruler – Trotsky and Stalin (see **A**). Lenin had feared that there would be a struggle for power between the two men. In his will Lenin warned that Stalin:

❛ . . . is too rude, and this fault . . . becomes unbearable in the office of General Secretary. Therefore, I propose to the comrades (members) to find a way to remove Stalin, and

D Stalin and Trotsky: strengths and weaknesses

Stalin

1 He was General Secretary of the Communist Party, and able to control its quickly-growing membership.
2 He was pleasant to opposing groups in the government . . . 'Next entered Zinoviev. He passed by Trotsky, and both behaved as if they had not noticed one another . . . At last Stalin came in. He approached the table at which Trotsky was seated, greeted him in a most friendly manner and vigorously shook hands with him across the table.'
3 He had been a leading member of the Party since 1903, and played a central role in the 1917 revolution.
4 He was known to be rude and aggressive to people he disliked.
5 He was ruthless and willing to wipe out any enemies of the party.
6 He was a very good organiser, who loved running government departments.
7 He was not a thinker – he would often use the ideas of others, and put these forward as his own.

Trotsky

1 In 1924 he was in charge of the Red Army. He had run the army during the Civil War, and had no interest in running a government department.
2 He was a thinker, who pushed for the spreading of the revolution to other countries, like Germany.
3 He was a member of a small group which was cut off from the main bulk of Party members in the government.
4 He was feared, people felt he was too ambitious and might become a military dictator.
5 He was an ex-Menshevik who had only joined the Bolshevik party in mid-1917.
6 He had played a crucial role in the 1917 revolution, and had commanded the Red Guards which had routed Kerensky.
7 He was a brilliant orator who could get a crowd on his side. But he was also shy and unable to make close friends.

Trotsky		Stalin	
1879	Born, son of Jewish landowner.	**1879**	Born, son of a Georgian peasant who had become a cobbler. Father drunk and violent. Entered church school – narrow, religious education.
1888	Went to school in Odessa – modern, liberal education.		
1897–98	Becomes a Marxist, organises workers against bosses.	**1894**	Sent to a seminary to train as a priest. Becomes a socialist.
1900	After arrest and trial, exiled to Siberia.	**1899**	Expelled. Begins life as underground Marxist worker.
1902	Escapes from Siberia. Travels to Europe to join Lenin.	**1902–04**	Jailed, sent to Siberia.
1903	Marxists split into Bolsheviks and Mensheviks – Trotsky opposes Lenin's Bolsheviks.	**1904**	Becomes Bolshevik – supporter of Lenin.
1905	Trotsky leader of Petrograd Soviet during 1905 revolution.	**1905**	Leads group of revolutionary fighters in the Caucasus mountains.
1906–14	Leading Menshevik – continues split from Lenin.	**1906–14**	Continues as Bolshevik member, Leninist.
1914–17	Exiled in Europe and America, agrees with Lenin's ideas. *May* 1917 – returns to Petrograd. Joins Lenin to mount revolution.	**1912**	Member of Party's Central Committee.
		1913–17	Exiled to Siberia.
1917	Trotsky organises the Red Guards. *September* president of Petrograd Soviet.	**1917**	Stalin edits Pravda. Plays leading role in organising the revolution. *November* – becomes Commissar of Nationalities in Bolshevik government.
1918	Military Commissar – in charge of fighting the Red Army in the Civil War.	**1918**	Stalin has major part to play in Civil War. Helps defend Petrograd against Whites. Major rows with Trotsky over fighting of the war.
1922	Commissar of War.	**1922**	General Secretary of the party – in charge of its administration.

E Stalin and Trotsky: early careers

appoint another man . . . more patient, more loyal, more polite and more attentive to comrades, less likely to act on impulse. **(B)**

Lenin felt that Trotsky had:

‘ . . . outstanding abilities. Personally, he is, I think, the most able member of the present government Central Committee (the governing body). But, he is far too arrogant. **(C)**

D and **E** look at the strong and weak points of Stalin and Trotsky as future leaders of Russia.

In 1924 a fierce row broke out between Trotsky and other members of the government. Trotsky wanted to spread the revolution to other countries like Poland and Germany – his idea was for a ‘permanent revolution’. His enemies said that these were not the ideas of Lenin, and that Trotsky had always been Lenin's enemy. They wanted the revolution to be finished in Russia first, with the building up of a communist classless society. Stalin called this ‘socialism in one country’.

Trotsky had few backers in the Politburo. In January 1925 he lost his job in charge of the army, although he was still in the Politburo. Stalin tried to keep the peace. But now the Politburo was split over the key question of what to do about farming and industry.

Farming was the big problem. After 1917 the great estates had been split up among the peasants. In 1926 there were some 25 million peasant farms – 9 million more than there had been ten years before. But the peasants in 1926 were not growing enough food to feed the towns and cities. Some Politburo members wanted to solve the problem, by setting up huge state collective farms (*kolkhoz*) and giving them tractors, tools, seed and grain. They also pushed for plans to make industry expand as quickly as possible. Their enemies in the Politburo said that these plans would not work. Stalin, with a group of backers, held the balance between the two sides. In 1926 and 1927 the Politburo agreed to take things slowly, and carry on with the plans of the NEP.

Trotsky had allied with the backers of ‘collectivisation’ and ‘industrialisation’. Stalin and his supporters defeated them. By the end of 1927 Stalin had driven Trotsky out of the party. Stalin's middle group now ran the government, along with the men who had been Trotsky's enemies. All the time Stalin, as General Secretary, was giving key jobs in local and central government to men he could trust.

A major crisis in 1928 gave Stalin the chance to turn on Trotsky's enemies. The failure of the kulaks to provide grain for the towns became more serious. Stalin now backed plans for collectivisation. In 1928 and 1929 there were furious rows in the Politburo. Stalin's views won the day, and his enemies were forced out of office. By December 1929, Stalin's fiftieth birthday, he was in full charge of the party. Timechart **F** outlines his rise to power.

1924 *January* Lenin dies. Struggle for power between Trotsky and Stalin. Stalin allies with Kamenev and Zinoviev – they form the *Triumvirate*. Trotsky fails to go to Lenin's funeral.
April Stalin's book *Foundations of Leninism* provides a guide to Communism for new party members. Triumvirate carry on NEP and oppose 'permanent revolution'.

1925 *January* Trotsky replaced as Commissar for War. Kamenev and Zinoviev back collectivisation and industrialisation.
December Kamenev and Zinoviev attack Stalin at 14th Congress of the Bolshevik Party. They are defeated by 559 votes to 65. Stalin's backers Molotov, Voroshilov and Kalinin join Politburo. Kamenev removed from Politburo.

1926 *January* Trotsky, Kamenev and Zinoviev ally against Stalin and the right wing of the party. Try to gain backing in the army but the plan is found out.

1927 *July* Zinoviev removed from Politburo. Stalin removes Zinoviev's supporters in Leningrad Party (Zinoviev's headquarters).
October Trotsky, Zinoviev and Kamenev admit they were wrong to plot against the party. Trotsky and Kamenev removed from Politburo.
7 November Zinoviev and Trotsky head demonstrations in Moscow and Leningrad against Stalin. Both removed from party a week later.
December Supporters of Trotsky, Zinoviev, Kamenev expelled from party.

1928 *January* Trotsky sent to live in exile at Alma Ata.
January–February Stalin leads party officials in raid on kulaks in Urals and Siberia. They force kulaks to hand over grain to the government.
April–June Stalin controls majority on Politburo. Removes all who oppose plans to force kulaks to hand over grain. Gains support from backers of Kamenev and Zinoviev by attacking right-wing opposition led by Bukharin.

1929 *December* Bukharin loses post as editor of *Pravda*. Stalin now in full control of the party. Removes all remaining opponents. Trotsky expelled from Russia.

??????????????????

1 Make notes on each of the following: Lenin's will; triumvirate; 'permanent revolution'; 'socialism in one country'; collectivisation; Kamenev and Zinoviev; Trotsky.

2 a Look back at the beginning of this section. In pairs or small groups, put points 1–5 into your order of importance for choosing someone to run your school.
b Beside each point say which of the rival leaders, Stalin or Trotsky, was most likely to have had that quality when he was at school. What makes you think so?

3 Divide into pairs. One of you take the part of a Stalin supporter in 1924, the other a backer of Trotsky. Use the points in lists **D** and **E** to convince the other that your leader was the right person to rule Russia in 1924.

4 *Essay title* How did Stalin gain power? Use the evidence in this section and anything else you can find to answer this question. (Think about; ruthlessness; death of rivals; tactics; policies and views; rivals; Trotsky's role; reasonableness; giving jobs to his friends.) You can use each of the following sentences to start a paragraph in your essay:

1 In arguments Stalin always appeared reasonable and took the middle ground.
2 Stalin's ruthlessness became apparent to his rival too late.
3 Stalin used his role as General Secretary to build up a party membership which was loyal to him.
4 When he had to, Stalin was willing to change his plans and policies, and even adopt those of his rivals.
5 Stalin was a master of tactics in in-fighting, and used meetings of the Central Committee to push through his schemes.
6 Trotsky's character played a big part in enabling Stalin to succeed.
7 In 1924 Stalin was one of a group of rivals on the Politburo who spent time and energy fighting one another.
8 The deaths of Stalin's rivals cleared his path to power.

18 Collectivisation

‘*Wipe out the kulaks (rich peasants) as a class . . . Should kulaks be allowed to join collective farms? Of course not, for they are the sworn enemies of the collective farm (kolkhoz) movement.*’ (**A**)
(Stalin, December 1929)

By the end of 1929 government attempts to change Russian farming were having little success. In 1929 Russia's farms grew less than in 1913. In the towns and cities food was short. For Russia's industry to expand, agriculture had to produce more raw materials and surplus food for the factory workers and their families. Russia needed to sell surplus food abroad to pay for new machines and to employ experts to train Russian factory workers. So Stalin had to try and increase the amount of grain, vegetables, meat and crops grown on Russia's peasant farms.

Collective farms were Stalin's answer. In 1929 only 100 peasant farms belonged to a collective farm or *kolkhoz*. To form a kolkhoz the peasants pooled all their private farmland, animals and machinery. These were now owned by the State. The peasants only kept small vegetable plots for themselves. A committee of peasants and government farming experts ran the kolkhoz and farmed its land (**B**).

Stalin's speech of December 1929 (see **A**) led to attempts to collectivise many of Russia's 200 000 villages in the next three months. Central to the plan to set up kolkhoz was an attack on the rich peasants, or *kulaks*. Stalin was sure that the kulaks were stopping the poor peasants from joining their local kolkhoz. Early in 1930 Stalin sent bands of Communist Party members from the cities to set up kolkhoz in the countryside.

What did joining a kolkhoz involve? Maurice Hindus was an American who had been born and raised in a Russian village. When he went back to his village it had become a kolkhoz. What did this mean for the peasant farmers?

‘*Gone were the long strips with their grassy furrows and ridges, stretching out to the horizon . . . There lay before me an immense field . . . Not all the peasants had joined the kolkhoz — that was clear from the small field on the opposite side of the road.*

. . . The rye on the land of the kolkhoz was gorgeous, tall, clean, heavily-eared and in even rows, clearly sown not by the irregular human hand but by the mathematically controlled grain drill . . . the spring crops (were) on the other side of the road — potatoes, barley, oats and large patches of flax, all so high that they hid the earth with their sweep of green.’ (**C**)

B How a kolkhoz (collective) was set up (based on a model kolkhoz visited by Maurice Hindus)

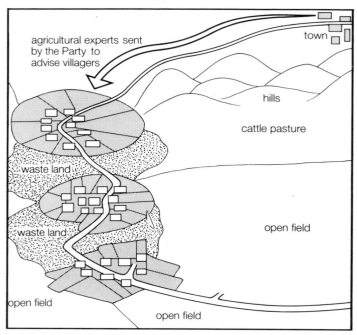

How a collective was set up (based on a model kolkhoz).

a On a visit to the village a group of Communist Party members (brigadiers) would organise the kolkhoz.

b The brigade stripped kulaks of their land, homes, animals and property.

c Poor peasants could keep their own plots of land or join the kolkhoz, which had the village's best land.

d A committee of poor peasants ran the kolkhoz with help from party members and farming experts.

e The committee built: new houses in rows; food silos; four cattle barns, each for 150 cows; a piggery, with 250 sows; a shop; a hospital; a nursery; a schoolhouse and a hen hatchery.

f The peasants worked the kolkhoz lands in labour gangs.

From the fields Maurice went on to the village:

‘*Houses, yards, fences, were in sad need of repair. Was this neglect a mere accident? The village boomed with life. From all directions people were returning from work, with sickles and hoes on their shoulders, with sacks of weeds, food for the pigs, and with loads of firewood on their backs . . . Young people were leading or driving cows from pasture. Kolkhoz teams with groups of workers were clattering along the streets.*’ (**D**)

Maurice was able to talk to the peasants about the kolkhoz. In the village was a 'brigade' of Communist Party members and students, to help run the kolkhoz.

why decided to organise Russias peasants 35 into collective farms.

Outside the blacksmith's Maurice stopped to talk to friends. Soon a crowd formed. A fierce row broke out between peasants against the kolkhoz and those in favour – the *kolkhozniks*:

❝Old man *One thing at least we have now learned is not to keep more than one cow or horse and at most only two pigs and a few sheep. They have taught us a lesson, one that we shall not forget soon.*❞ (E)

❝Little man *A party of those special brigadiers* (students/soldiers/party members) *paid me a visit the other day. . . . one of them came back to find out if I was a kulak. I have an old straw cutter with which I have been earning 10 or 15 miserable roubles a year – well, I was charged with being an exploiter. It is a rusty old thing, this cutter, I have had it for 15 years. So when the brigadier suggested that I was making money out of people, I laughed and told him that he could have the whole machine for the price of the iron in it . . .* (the little man is asked about his cow. His wife comes in and shouts at the brigadier). *Once she spat at him. I was fairly scared.*❞ (F)

❝Nikolai *Last year, I thought of joining the kolkhoz, but my wife threatened to kill herself if I did, so I did not. Well, you see me as I stand here? That's how they left me. Everything else they took away, except three poods* (1 pood = 3.1 lb) *of grain and a few sacks of potatoes which they allowed me to keep as a favour.*

(*Another peasant added:* "*the finest pair of horses in the village, three cows, ten sheep, 20 hens, a wagon, ploughs, they stripped him of everything and drove him out of his own house, in freezing weather. Merciless.*")❞ (G)

❝Kolkhoznik 1 *Every time anything happens in the kolkhoz they yell themselves hoarse about it. They forget the same things happen outside the kolkhoz. One of our men tipped over a load of hay, and it was the talk of the whole countryside for weeks.*❞ (H)

❝Kolkhoznik 2 *What a life in the kolkhoz, always under someone's orders! Yesterday, for instance, I did not work. I just wanted a rest so I took one, and I ate more than I usually do, five times as much.*❞ (J)

❝Kolkhoznik 3 *When the harvest comes it will all be different. We'll have more than any of you and we'll fare and live better. Just you wait and see, all you grousers.*❞ (K)

❝Ilya *Would that be anything unusual? You have got the best land in the village, the best pasture, the best grain for seed, the best horses, cows and pigs, raised by decent people with their own sweat and blood in this and other villages. You have wood and timber from the State forest, tractors and other machines, money from the government . . . Where then will the miracle be : . . Get the poorest land you can find, let the government put on you half the burdens that it puts on us, do everything with your own hands, and see then what you can do.*❞ (L)

❝Student *The kulak has to be got out of the way as fully as the enemy at the front. He is the enemy at the front. He is the enemy of the kolkhoz . . . What pity did these same kulaks show to women and children when they had their bins loaded with rye and wheat and would let none go to the city, where . . . millions of women and children were threatened with starvation?*❞ (M)

Maurice paid his visit in March 1930. The process of setting up the kolkhozs and 'de-kulakisation' had caused death and misery in many villages. Kulaks were forced to live on waste land, or shipped by train to work as forced labour, building canals or factories. Eugene Lyons was a foreign reporter in Russia. He described a train loaded with kulaks:

❝*Small openings high up at one end of the freight cars were the only source of air and light for the hundreds of men, women and children jammed into the prison cars. These openings were now crowded with peasant faces, craning for a view of the station full of foreigners: weary, hopeless faces deeply ingrained with dirt.*❞ (N)   (Eugene Lyons *Assignment in Utopia*, 1937)

The kolkhoz movement went on from 1930 to 1934, by which time half of Russia's villages were collectivised. Everywhere, better-off peasants refused to take part. They killed their horses and cows, hid their grain and failed to sow the crops. The result was a massive famine, from 1932–33:

❝*The most terrifying sights were the little children with skeleton limbs dangling from balloon-like abdomens. Starvation had wiped every trace of youth from their faces, turning them into tortured gargoyles. Only in their eyes lingered the reminder of childhood. Everywhere we found men and women lying prone, their faces and bellies bloated.*❞ (O)   (Victor Kravchenko, *I Choose Freedom*, 1947)

Eugene Lyons goes on:

❝*The sight of peasants being led by soldiers with drawn revolvers through even the streets of Moscow was too commonplace even to win more than a casual glance from the crowds on the sidewalks. I talked to refugees who came to our doors to beg a few crumbs of bread . . .*❞ (P)

By 1934 some five million had died of hunger. Another three million kulaks had been sent to die in the labour camps. *Why such terrible consequences collectivisation*

From 1935 the kolkhoz movement began to produce better results, as **Q** shows. Timechart **R** outlines the process of collectivisation.

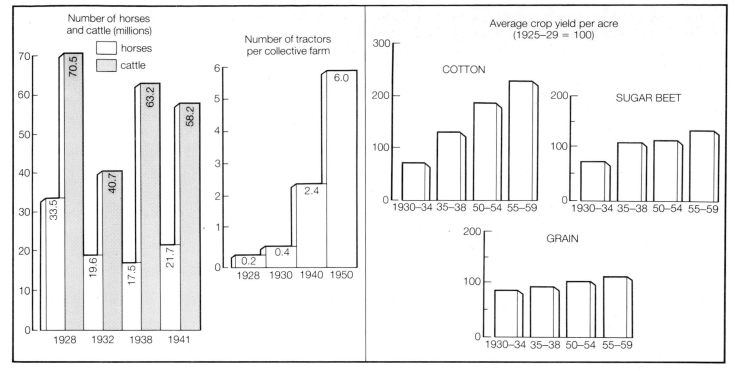

Q The effects of collectivisation on output

R Timechart: 1917–37

1917	Peasants took over landed estates, and split them up into peasant farms. Private ownership.
1927–28	Drop in grain prices in 1926–27, led to shortage of grain in 1927, as peasants sowed less.
1928	*January–February* Stalin led police and army raid on peasants in Urals and Siberia and forced them to hand over grain.
1928–29	Arguments over how quickly to extend collective and state farms (giant state-owned farms were known as Sovkhoz). Only 2% of peasants in collective or state farms.
1929	*December–March 1930* 55% of farms collectivised.
1930	*1 March* Stalin called halt to collectivisation. Peasants allowed own plots. Kulaks had been wiped out. *1 June* Only 23% of peasants in collectives.
1931–33	Stalin pressed on with collectivisation plans. Mass slaughtering of animals. Passive resistance of peasants.
1931/32	Widespread famine.
1934–37	Recovery of farming. Peasants produced vegetables, fruit, meat, milk on their private plots. Grain, cotton, sugar beet and flax came from kolkhoz and Sovkhoz land. Motor Tractor Stations (MTS), provided machinery from a central depot for the working of kolkhoz land.
1937	Most farms collectivised.

??????????????

1 Complete the following sentences:
In 1917 the Russian peasant gained control over . . .
From 1918–28 farming was in the hands of . . .
By 1929 the kolkhoz movement had been . . .
In December 1929 . . .
March 1930 saw . . .
The move to wipe out the kulaks meant . . .
In 1932–33 there was . . .
By 1937 . . .
A kolkhoz was . . .
A Sovkhoz was . . .

2 As if you were members of the kolkhoznik committee in charge of village **B**, plan out how you would collectivise it, carrying out points *b–f*. Keep a diary of your decisions, what happened at meetings and in the village, and how your plans were carried out. (You can work in pairs, groups or as a whole class.)

3 If Maurice had returned to his village in March 1933, what might the following tell him has happened in the past three years: Old man; Little man; Nikolai; Kolkhozniks 1, 2, 3; Ilya; student?

4 What trust can we place on sources **C–M**; **N**; **O**; as historical evidence. (Think about who produced it; when; why; how? What sort of evidence is it?)

19 Industrialisation

❝To slow down the speed of industrialisation means to lag behind. And those who lag behind are beaten. The history of Old Russia shows that because she was backward she was being defeated all the time . . . Beaten because she was backward – military, cultural, political, industrial and agricultural backwardness . . ✳*We are behind the leading countries by 150 years. We must make up this distance in ten years. Either we do it or we go under*✳❞ (A) Use in Stalin Essays.

So Stalin argued during the first *Five Year Plan* (1928–32). The FYP set targets for increases in the making of iron, steel, heavy machinery and chemicals (see **B** and **C**). Gosplan, the government's economic planning body, planned the FYP and ran it from Moscow. Gosplan decided every detail of what Russia's industry should make, and what would happen to factories' products. Gosplan planned new towns like Magnitogorsk; the building of new factories in old

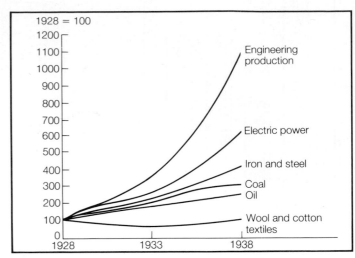

C Russian industrial output 1928–38 (official figures)

industrial centres like the Donetz Basin (Donbass); and huge dams like the Dnieper Dam, to provide hydro-electric power for the new factories.

Stalin claimed that the first FYP had achieved its goals in four years. So he announced a second FYP (1933–37). It aimed to run the factories of the first FYP more efficiently, and to provide some consumer goods for the workers.

Louis Fischer, an American, visited Russia in 1935. The following extracts come from his book, *Soviet Journey*. If, in 1935, you had visited Russia with Louis Fischer, what might you have seen of Russia's new industries?

❝Moscow is encircled by a broad ring of new factories, and housing estates. Eight miles from the heart of the city stands the Freezer Cutting Tool Plant finished in 1931. In sight of it are six new factories . . . From the outside it looks like a modern European or American factory, but on its walls, in large letters, slogans have been painted, "Long live the World Revolution".❞ (D)

From Moscow you take a train to see the Dnieper Dam (**E**). The Dnieper Dam has been built to solve three problems:

1 the shortage of electricity in the area;

2 the difficulty of using the river for shipping;

3 the shortage of water for local farmers during the crop growing season.

When you talk to the foreman at the dam (**F**) you learn:

B Timechart: 1928–41

1928	First Five Year Plan. Targets set to double output in key heavy industries – coal, iron and steel, chemicals, heavy engineering.
1929	*December* FYP to be completed in four years.
1929–32	New cities like Magnitogorsk, Komsomolsk, founded. Urals, Kuzbass, Volga River industrial areas set up. Expansion of industry in traditional areas around Moscow, Leningrad and in Donetz Basin (Donbass). Dnieper Hydro-electric Dam completed (Europe's largest) rail and canal links built between main industrial centres. *Gosplan* – state control of all aspects of economic life: making, transporting and selling. Free medical care, health insurance and education in evening classes for workers.
1931	Targets set for each worker, to which wages linked. Dismissal for absenteeism. Slackers sent to labour camps. Death for stealing state property.
1933–37	Second FYP. Continues pattern of first plan, but aims to improve efficiency. Higher priority given to consumer goods.
1935	*August* Stakhanov mines 102 tonnes of coal in five hours – 14 times target. Stakhanovite movement – groups of similar workers set targets for other industries, held as models for other workers.
1936	Stalin introduces new 'democratic' Constitution. Russia to be ruled by Council of Ministers (itself controlled by Stalin). Only Communist candidates allowed in elections.
1938–41	Third FYP. 1940 labour laws give government complete control over worker's lives. Increasing emphasis on education – from 1928–40 there were 291 000 Engineering and Industrial graduates; 103 400 Agricultural qualifications.

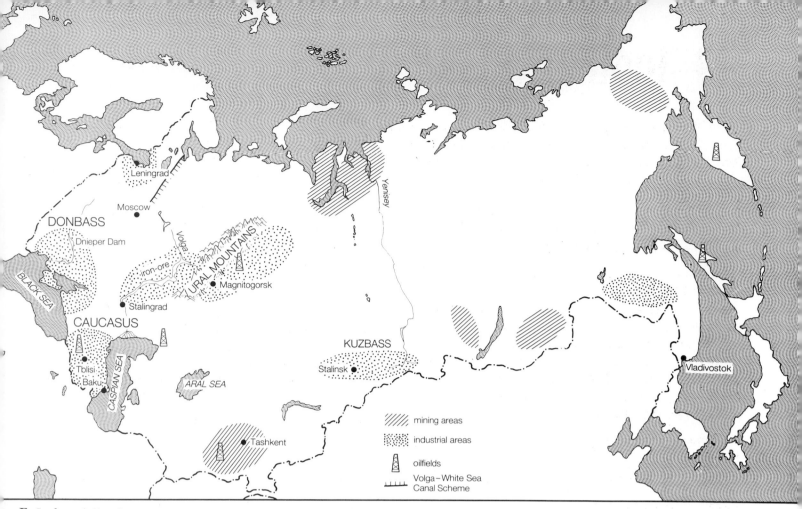

E Industrialisation

‘The Dnieper hydro-electric power station's output is 600 000 kilowatts. But the factories in and around Zaporozhie (a local town) will never be able to use more than half of this amount. To consume the balance, a 200 kilometre long, high tension line must be built to the iron mines of Krivoi Rog; another, 120 kilometres long to the Donetz coalfield, and still another to the manganese deposits at Nikopol. During the months when the water in the Dnieper is low, however, these remote districts will depend on their local power resources . . .’ (G)

You go on to see the dam itself:

‘Where the dam ends, three huge locks have been cut out of solid granite. This makes the Dnieper navigable from the Black Sea all the way to Smolensk in White Russia. On the Dnieper near Kiev (there were) timber rafts being floated downstream from the woodlands of North-Western Russia to the treeless prairies of the Ukraine. But that is just the point. The Dnieper is only navigable to timber rafts and river barges. 60 miles above the dam, the Dnieper becomes shallow again. To open the river to deep-draught sea-going vessels, the Bolsheviks propose to construct three more dams along the Dnieper in the next five years and ten more by 1950. (The Nikopol manganese mines output has gone up 6 times in the last six years.) But now plans have been made to carry the ore from the mines to the river and then transfer it to barges. (A 4/5s saving of transport costs over rail haulage.)’ (H)

The dam provides electricity for a local new town:

‘In 1931 wheat still grew where the factories now stand. An industrial centre at this point enjoys the advantages of cheap local electric power and of closeness to the coal of the Donetz coal basin and the iron of Krivoi Rog. Besides, there is cheap water transport. Only a fraction of the plant is now ready, but the city is already a busy metal centre. The aluminium works are producing goods which, unfortunately do not reach Soviet citizen's kitchens. You visit a blast furnace, and in just 30 seconds you are: choking, breathless, out of action . . . How can men stand it six hours a day? ".They get used to it". It's like getting used to live on rat poison. "Can't they wear gas masks?" Under a truly socialist regime, these victims will work two hours a day and then be taken for rides in open aeroplanes.’ (J)

The new town is built:

‘. . . near the river — the factories are several kilometres further inland . . . The streets are broad avenues lined with trees and lawns. The houses are good, two or one storey dwellings with big windows, much electric light, white inside and out. *The new city — it has a population of 15 000 — boasts a theatre, several cinemas, two clubhouses, a Park of Culture and Rest, a small sports stadium, schools etc. It is well planned. But there is no planning for the future. No space for garages, for example.* **(K)**

After you leave the Dnieper Dam you visit Karkhov, the Ukraine's biggest city:

'*The population of Karkhov rose from 288 000 in 1917 to 380 000 in 1926, to 836 000 in 1934. Many complete blocks of houses stand out as fresh and modern. Smokestacks show that numerous factories operate within the city. But most of the large industrial works put up by the Bolsheviks during and since the First Five Year Plan are placed far from the centre of town. Thus the Karkhov Tractor Factory is some 12 kilometres from the city. (You visit it) As one looks over the great assembly room — the eye cannot see its end — each person is obviously doing his job and working quite hard. The plant*

F The Dnieper Dam

employed 11 000 in 1932 when it was making 50 tractors a day, and employs 11 500 at present when it makes 145 per day. **(L)**

You leave Karkhov to return to Moscow:

The train cuts through the heart of the Donetz coal basin . . . A powerful, metal, chemical and cement industry is growing up in this region. Everywhere, new works and new homes. At Kramatorsk – on one side of the track, a new Soviet metallurgical giant which produces heavy factory equipment, bought before from abroad. It began working in the Autumn of 1934. On the other side of the track, mud thatched huts, mud streets, peasants. **(M)**

???????????????

1 What does **C** suggest about production: of consumer goods; by heavy industry, between 1928 and 1938?

2 If you visited the factory in **D** in 1931, what might the foreman tell you about: his orders from Gosplan; problems of getting raw materials for the works; building materials; labour force; use of works' output when finished?

3 Write short paragraphs on: Gosplan; first FYP; Dnieper Dam; Donbass; Stakhanov; Karkhov Tractor Factory; industrial growth 1928–38.

Planner

It is 1929. You are a member of Gosplan. You have to plan the industrial growth of area **X** (see map). The area has a large peasant population and no proper roads. What would you suggest?

First make out a table like the one below. Fill in your target for each year (percentage growth).

For example, if you want coal production to go up by 20 per cent in the first year, put 20 per cent under Year 1.

When you have made out your plan, throw a die to see how well you get on. Look at the *Progress chart* to find out what happens for each score. Which industries are involved? How important are they? How does this affect industrial growth in the area?

Note down the results of each throw. Has your Three Year Plan been a success or a failure?

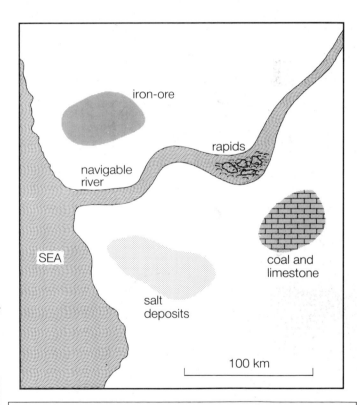

	Year 1	Year 2	Year 3
Coal			
Iron			
Chemicals			
Power			
Roads			
Railways			
Canals			
Town/Housing			
Services (schools etc)			
Labour force			

Progress chart

1 Explosion in iron works destroys smelter – no iron produced that year

2 Delays in building canals and railways stops supplies reaching building sites

3 Flooding washes away main railway line and roads, and destroys half completed hydro-electric dam

4 Severe winter cuts output of hydro-electric scheme, failure of local factories to reach production targets

5 Arrest of engineers in chemical works mean that they are shut for six months – no output

6 Typhoid breaks out in the local towns – labour force dies in huge numbers, drop in output from the factories

20 The Great Terror

You go home tonight. Later, while you are fast asleep, one of your family wakes you up, saying:

> *"We have visitors." You spring out of bed to see a soldier in the hall. Two NKVD (secret police) officers in uniform are in your sitting room . . . The secret police officers forbid you to speak to one another.* **(A)**

(Betty Garland, *Caviar for Breakfast*, 10 April 1936)

All night the secret police search your home. In the morning they take your parents away. You never see them again. What might happen to your parents at the secret police's headquarters?

> *I was put on the "conveyor belt". The interrogators worked in shifts: I didn't. Seven days without sleep or food. The object of the conveyor is to wear out nerves, weaken the body, break resistance, and force the prisoner to sign whatever is required.* (**One interrogator**) *"Ha, ha, ha! What's become of our high-brow beauty now! You look at least 40 . . . You haven't been in the rubber cell yet, have you? You haven't? Well, that's a pleasure in store."*
>
> *Major Elshin (a second interrogator) was always polite and "humane". He liked talking about my children . . .* **(B)**

C A Russian political prison (based on the only known map, drawn by a prisoner)

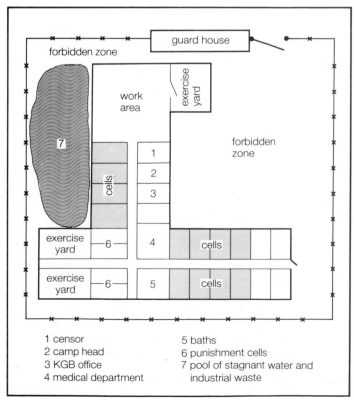

1 censor
2 camp head
3 KGB office
4 medical department
5 baths
6 punishment cells
7 pool of stagnant water and industrial waste

D Timechart: The Great Terror: 1928–53

1928–33	Number of show trials – including that of British *Vickers* engineers accused of sabotage.
1934	*December* Shooting of Kirov leads to Great Terror. 1100 out of 1900 delegates to the 1933 Bolshevik Party Conference die.
1935	Leningrad branch of the party wiped out. Mass arrests throughout Russia.
1936	First great show trial of Bolshevik party leaders – Kamenev and Zinoviev (see page 42).
1937	Second show trial. Arrest of army and navy commanders.
1938	Third show trial – Bukharin and Rykov (Bukharin had been a party ruler in the 1920s along with Stalin and Trotsky). Also on trial was Yagoda, head of the Secret Police until 1936.
	Those on trial were accused of: a treasonable plot with Trotsky to overthrow Stalin; plots in early 1920s to murder Lenin and Stalin; spying for Germany and Japan; plans to sabotage Russia's economy by attacking factories and railways. All the accused confessed.
	About six million in labour camps – building Volga–White Sea Canal or working in Siberia. (70% of labour force kulaks.)
1945	Two million Russians who returned to Russia after the War sent to labour camps. 100 000 party members purged each year.
1949	Arrest of party leadership in Leningrad (all killed).
1953	'Doctors' plot' – doctors who treated Stalin were accused of plans to murder him. *March* Death of Stalin.

Once they had confessed, your parents might be shot or sent to a labour or prison camp like **C**. Few came out alive. Between 1934 and 1953 millions of Russians were arrested (see **D**).

In December 1934 a gunman shot and killed Kirov, head of the Leningrad branch of the Bolshevik Party. There is a strong possibility that Stalin had him killed. Stalin then used Kirov's death as a reason to arrest members of the party whom he thought were his enemies. The 'terror' swept up millions of Russians from all walks of life (**E**). In 1936 began the first of a series of great 'show trials' of the men who had ruled Russia along with Stalin in the 1920s. In 1937 the commander-in-chief of the army, General Tukhashevsky, was arrested. The *purges* spread to all ranks of the army and navy. After World War II millions of Russians who had been taken prisoner by the Germans or had helped them were sent to the labour camps. Party purges went on up to Stalin's death in 1953. He was the greatest mass murderer in the world's history.

E Figures from the 1959 official census. After allowing for war losses, figures are some 20 million lower than expected

Age	Born	Numbers (thous.)		Percentage	
		Male	*Female*	*Male*	*Female*
0– 9	1950+	23 608	22 755	50.9	49.1
10–19	1940+	16 066	15 742	50.5	49.5
20–24	1935+	10 056	10 287	49.4	50.6
25–29	1930+	8 917	9 273	49.0	51.0
30–34	1925+	8 611	10 388	45.3	54.7
35–39	1920+	4 528	7 062	39.1	60.9
40–44	1915+	3 998	6 410	38.4	61.6
45–49	1910+	4 706	7 558	38.4	61.6
50–54	1905+	4 010	6 437	38.4	61.6
55–59	1900+	2 906	5 793	33.4	66.6
60–69	1895+	4 099	7 637	34.9	65.1
70 and older		2 541	5 431	31.9	68.1
Total		94 050	114 777	45.0	55.0

??????????????????

1 What was/who were: NKVD; the conveyor belt; Yagoda; Kirov; Tukhashevsky; Bukharin; a show trial; the doctor's plot; Volga–White Sea Canal; 1959 census?

2 What impact did the Great Terror have on:
  a The Party members (**D**)?
  b Party leaders of the 1920s (**D**)?
  c Men in their 30s and 40s (1933–41) (**E**)?

3 Betty Garland's husband died in a labour camp in 1938. What might she be able to tell you about what happened to her husband after his arrest? (Use **A**, **B** and **C** to help you.)

4 a Write a paragraph explaining what you know of 'The Great Terror'.
  b Why did Stalin carry out 'The Great Terror'?
  c Why do you think many people confessed?

5 *Classroom terror* The huge number of arrests during The Great Terror followed on from arrested people telling the police about others who were plotting. Imagine that the NKVD (your teacher) is questioning your form. You have all been asked to 'confess' your crimes, and tell what you know of other people's crimes. These crimes are against the school – how you work, treat teachers and fellow pupils.

Write down your accusations on a piece of paper and give it to the NKVD. The NKVD can arrest up to five members of the form using the *evidence* he or she now has. Then the evidence against the arrested is read out. Form members discuss and write down what they know about these accusations. The accused can tell what they know about the others under arrest.

21 Foreign Policy

The main aim of a country's foreign policy is to defend its interests. One of Lenin's chief goals was to bring about a world Communist revolution. To spread Communist ideas and help plan revolutions he set up an organisation called the Communist International (or *Comintern*) in 1919 (**A**).

Other countries distrusted Russia – she was an international outcast. Russia took no part in the Versailles Peace Conference. Lenin knew that Russia, surrounded by Capitalist countries, would have to struggle to survive. In 1922 Russia signed the Treaty of Rapallo with Germany, the other 'outcast' of Europe.

Lenin died in 1924. Under Stalin, Soviet foreign policy changed. Stalin believed the Soviet Union must first be made strong, before it could help Communist revolution in other countries. He aimed to strengthen the Soviet economy through Five Year Plans. Stalin

A Main treaties and events 1918–37

1918	Treaty of Brest–Litovsk – land lost to Germany.
1919	Comintern set up.
1921	Treaty of Riga – ended Polish–Russian War. Trade treaties with Britain.
1922	Treaty of Rapallo – Germany lent the USSR money. A secret clause let Germany make weapons in Russia.
1927	Stalin lost influence with the Nationalist Party in China when Sun Yatsen came to power.
1928	Kellogg–Briand Pact – 65 countries, including Russia, promised not to use war to settle disputes.
1931	Fighting against Japan in Manchuria.
1932	Friendship treaties with Poland and France.
1934	The USSR joined the League of Nations.
1935	The USSR, France and Czechoslovakia agreed to help each other if attacked.
1936–39	Spanish Civil War.
1936	Anti-Comintern Pact – Germany and Japan. Italy joined in 1937. Spain joined in 1939.
1937	Soviet and Japanese troops fought on the border of Manchuria.
1939	*August* Nazi–Soviet Pact.
	1 September Germany attacked Poland.
	3 September Britain and France declared war on Germany.
	17 September Russia invaded eastern Poland as agreed with Germany.
	October Stalin forced Latvia, Lithuania and Estonia to allow Soviet troops to enter their territory.
	November The 'Winter War' began – Soviet troops attacked Finland when the Finns refused to exchange some land Stalin wanted to improve Russia's defences.
1940	*February* The Finns surrendered.

believed in 'Socialism in One Country' before 'World Revolution'. He explained:

❝ *Our country is encircled by capitalism. It is impossible to preserve our independence without having an adequately industrialised base for defence . . . the capitalist countries will do all in their power to crush communist countries.* ❞ **(B)**

In the 1930s real problems began to appear for Stalin. In 1931 Japan invaded Manchuria, on Russia's eastern border. (You can read more about this in *Modern China* in this series.) Then in 1933 Hitler came to power in Germany. Hitler hated Communism. He saw parts of Soviet Russia as possible living space *(Lebensraum)* for Germans. In his book *Mein Kampf* he warned:

❝ *We turn our eyes to the East* (Russia and Poland) *it is ripe for destruction . . . The future goal of our foreign policy ought to have in view the gaining of such Eastern territory as is necessary for our German people.* ❞ **(C)**

By 1935 Stalin had ordered the Comintern to begin a 'Popular Front against Fascism'. Communist parties abroad were to help other left-wing parties to stop the spread of Nazism and other Fascist movements. But in 1936 the first Anti-Comintern Pact (an anti-Communist

agreement) was signed. The same year, General Franco led a Fascist revolt in Spain against the Republican Government. Germany and Italy helped Franco. Stalin sent aid to the Republicans.

By 1938 the danger to Russia of invasion was growing. In eastern Russia extra Soviet troops were needed to watch the Japanese. But the much greater threat was the growing power of Germany in the west. Hitler had begun to build up a German Empire and wanted parts of Soviet Russia.

In September 1938 Britain and France signed the Munich Agreement giving Hitler the Sudetenland. Stalin believed this was proof that Britain and France were encouraging Hitler to attack Russia. A Russian schoolbook explains this view:

❝ *By handing over Czechoslovakia to Hitler, the ruling classes of England and France hoped that he* (Hitler) *had received enough payment to give up his aggression in Western Europe and that now he would surely start a war against the Soviet Union.* ❞ **(D)**

It was clear that Poland was next on Hitler's list and then, probably, Russia. Russia was not ready for war. Many Red Army officers had been killed in Stalin's purges and much of the army's equipment was out of date. What could Stalin do to protect Russia? He invited Britain and France to talk about an alliance against Hitler, but Britain had little confidence in Russia and the talks broke down. So on 23 August Russia signed a non-aggression pact with Germany. They agreed not to declare war on each other and, in a secret clause, to split Poland between them.

From September 1939 events moved quickly. By June 1940 Hitler controlled most of Western Europe (see **E**). Meanwhile, Stalin had ordered an urgent programme of retraining for the Red Army and Air Force.

E The Russian border and Central Europe 1939–41

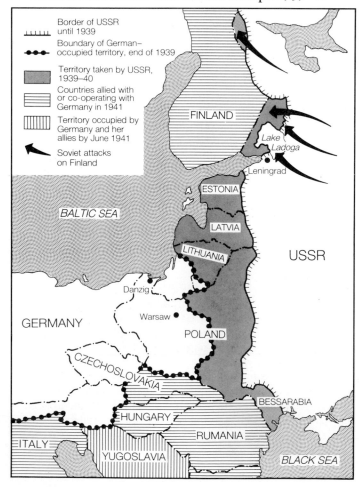

Border of USSR until 1939

Boundary of German-occupied territory, end of 1939

Territory taken by USSR, 1939–40

Countries allied with or co-operating with Germany in 1941

Territory occupied by Germany and her allies by June 1941

Soviet attacks on Finland

FINLAND

Lake Ladoga

Leningrad

BALTIC SEA

ESTONIA

LATVIA

LITHUANIA

USSR

Danzig

GERMANY

Warsaw

POLAND

CZECHOSLOVAKIA

BESSARABIA

HUNGARY

RUMANIA

ITALY

YUGOSLAVIA

BLACK SEA

??????????????

1 Make notes on: Comintern; the Rapallo Treaty; Lebensraum; the Popular Front; the Munich Agreement; 'Socialism in One Country'; the Winter War.

2 What advantages did the non-aggression pact give the USSR?

3 How might the Russian version of the Munich Agreement (**D**) differ from that in an English school textbook? Why?

4 Write an essay with the title: 'Stalin was only concerned with defending Russia.' (Use the points in question 1 to help you.)

22 Barbarossa

4.00 am, 22 June 1941 German bombs and shells destroy Russian towns, airfields and fuel and supply dumps. The German army attacks and bursts through the weak Russian defences. *Operation Barbarossa*, the German invasion of Russia, has begun. It comes as a surprise to Stalin. The Red Army is not ready for war. Yet there have been many warning signs.

At first Stalin seemed to lose his nerve, but on 3 July he spoke on the radio and urged people to resist:

❛*The enemy is cruel. He is out to seize our lands, our grain and oil. He is out to restore the rule of the landlords and to restore tsarism . . . to turn the Russians into the slaves of the Germans.*❜ (A)

He told the army and people to follow a 'scorched earth policy'. This meant leaving behind nothing that could be of any use to the invader:

❛*The enemy must not be left a single engine, railway car, pound of grain or gallon of fuel, all must be destroyed . . . In areas occupied by the enemy, guerilla groups must blow up bridges and roads, damage telephone and telegraph lines, set fire to forests, stores and transports . . . conditions must be made unbearable for the enemy.*❜ (B)

Stalin began to prepare Russia for a long war. More than 1500 factories in the path of the German advance were taken apart and moved by rail, with their workers, to safety in central and eastern Russia. A Russian newspaper told of how quickly new factories were built:

❛*The war factory had to start production in its new home in not more than 14 days. The people came with shovels, bars and pickaxes: students, typists, accountants, shop assistants, housewives, artists, teachers. The earth was like stone, frozen hard. People hacked at the earth all night . . . and laid the foundations . . . On the 14th day the war factory began production.*❜ (C)

The German army made three main thrusts: towards Leningrad in the north, Moscow in the centre, and Kiev and Rostov in the south (see map **D**). At first they advanced quickly. By November Leningrad was surrounded, Kiev was captured and the Germans were on the outskirts of Moscow. 2 million Russian soldiers had been captured.

Then the German army ran into problems. Rain had made many of the poor earth roads unusable. Then, in November, freezing weather froze German engines. Temperatures could be as low as −40°C. Without the right clothing and equipment for winter fighting, the German army slowed down. They made a desperate attempt to capture Moscow, but this failed.

Stalin strengthened Moscow's defences. Fresh troops were moved to the capital from Siberia when Stalin learned that the Japanese were planning to go to war against America and not Russia. Stalin stayed in Moscow to lead the fight against the Germans. In December 1941 the Russians pushed the German army back from Moscow.

D The German advance 1941

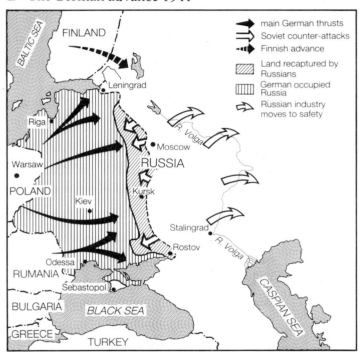

- → main German thrusts
- ⇒ Soviet counter-attacks
- ⊷ Finnish advance
- ▨ Land recaptured by Russians
- ⦀ German occupied Russia
- ⇨ Russian industry moves to safety

??????????????????

1 a In June 1941 what agreement did Hitler break (see page 44)?
b What is a 'scorched earth policy'?
c What did Stalin mean in **A** by 'restore tsarism'?

2 Draw a Russian *or* a German cartoon for December 1941, showing how the war is going.

3 a Why did Hitler find it so easy to invade Russia and almost defeat her in 1941? List all the reasons you can. Discuss your points with a partner, and put them in their order of importance.
b Compare your final list with that of another pair. Discuss the differences between your lists, and the reasons for them.

23 Leningrad

C Smouldering ruins in a Leningrad street

In 1941 Hitler said of Russia:

❝*We have only to kick in the door and the whole rotten structure will come down.*❞ **(A)**

He was wrong. In the end the door swung back and flattened the German army in the East. One place where the Germans kicked and kicked but did not get in was the city of Leningrad. German and Finnish troops surrounded the city in September 1941 and the greatest siege in modern history began. It lasted for two and a half years. This section looks at the siege, and how people lived and died in Leningrad.

In September 1941 Hitler ordered:

❝1 *The Führer has decided to wipe the City of Leningrad from the face of the earth. After the defeat of Soviet Russia there will be not the slightest reason for the future existence of this large city.*
2 *It is intended to blockade the city and destroy it by artillery fire and ceaseless bombardment from the air . . . if they want to surrender they will be refused . . . We have no interest in keeping even part of this great city's population.*❞ **(B)**

(German Directive No. 1a 1601/41)

Three million people lived in Leningrad. About one million of them died. This was more than the total British and American war dead.

Leningrad and the area around it was cut off from the rest of Russia. It could only be reached by the dangerous trip across Lake Ladoga (see map **E** on page 44). The Germans hammered away at the city. The Russians defended it bravely. Men, women and children all helped by fighting, digging defences and making weapons. The Germans could not break through. They decided to starve the city into surrender.

D Daily rations in Leningrad, 20 November

	Labourer	Child aged 8
	Grams	*Grams*
Bread	252	128
Fats	19	17
Meat	49	14
Cereals	49	39
Sugar	49	39
Total	418 = 4554 kilojoules	237 = 2865 kilojoules
Approximate daily need	14700 kilojoules	11760 kilojoules

How did the people live? It was difficult. There were plenty of ways of dying: enemy fire (see **C**), starvation, cold and disease. Food was scarce and had to be rationed. The ration was reduced five times. **D** shows what the daily ration was by 20 November. This is only a small part of what the human body needs. Deaths from starvation soared. Even this ration was not given in full, as there was not enough meat and fat. Substitutes like jelly made from sheep guts were used. In January 3500–4000 people were dying every day. People tried to eat anything:

To fill their empty stomachs people would try to catch crows, or any cat or dog that had still somehow survived; they would go through medicine chests in search of castor oil, hair oil, vaseline or glycerine, they would make up soup or jelly out of glue scraped off wallpaper or broken-up furniture . . . in the streets people would fall down and never rise again. (**E**)

There was also, of course, the danger of enemy shells or bombs (see **F**). One man recalled:

A shell landed close by and ten yards away from me was a man whose head was cut clean off by a shell splinter. It was horrible. I saw him make his last two steps already with his head off – and a bloody mess all around before he collapsed. I vomited. (**G**)

Daily life went on, if possible, but with no electricity or coal the hours of darkness were long and cold. Some schools stayed open. A 16-year-old schoolgirl, Luba, described what lessons were like:

Our classes continued on the "Round the Stove" principle. If you wanted a seat near the stove or under the stove pipe, you had to come early. It was agony to stand up and go to the blackboard . . . where it was cold and dark, and your hand,

imprisoned in its heavy glove, went all numb and rigid and refused to obey. The chalk kept falling out of your hand . . . By the time we reached the third lesson there was no more fuel left. The stove went cold and it became terribly cold. (**H**)

In November the weather got colder and Lake Ladoga froze. When the temperature reached $-15°C$ and the ice was two metres thick an ice road was made. Lorries began to bring in small amounts of food and take people out. Several lorries fell through the ice, but slowly the amount of food reaching the city grew. In January 1942 rations were increased, but it was another two years before the German stranglehold was broken.

It is difficult to really understand how such punishment affected people's lives. One personal tragedy may help: Tanya Savicheva, an 11-year-old girl, wrote what happened to her family on pages of her alphabetical notebook:

Z Zhenya died on 28th December, 12.30 in the morning, 1941. B Babushka died on 25th January, 3 o'clock, 1942. L Leka died on 17th March, 5 o'clock in the morning, 1942. D Dedya Vasya died on 13th April, 2 o'clock at night, 1942. D Dedya Lesha on 10th May, 4 o'clock in the afternoon, 1942. M Mama on 13th May, 7.30 am, 1942. S Savichers died. All died. Only Tanya remains. (**J**)

Sadly, Tanya herself, the only survivor in her family, was so weak she died of dysentry in 1943.

F Nevsky Prospect, Leningrad, under German bombardment

??????????????

1 a Describe what you can see at points **1–7** in **C** and **F**.
b What *can't* you see that you would expect to see in a normal city street? Why do you think this is?

2 a Why do you think the people of Leningrad did not surrender, despite the conditions?
b What evidence in **B** shows that they were right not to give in to the Germans?
c Why was the capture of Leningrad important to the Germans?

3 Look at **D**.
a Why do you think there was such a big difference between the rations of a labourer and a child?
b Approximately what percentage of their daily needs (in kilojoules) did each of them receive?

4 Imagine you are a young Russian trapped in Leningrad. Write a diary account for one day. (Mention: waking up, your feelings, your home, journey to work, your job, when to eat your ration, ideas for keeping warm, rumours, the dark, your family, death, sleep.)

24 The Impact of War

Winston Churchill said:

❝ *Nothing that has happened in the West can compare with the wholesale massacres not only of soldiers but of civilians and women and children in Hitler's invasion of Russia.* ❞ (**A**)

He was right. The war between the Soviet Union and Germany was different from the war between Germany and the Western Allies (Britain, France, USA and Canada). It was much more cruel. Hitler said it was a 'war of extermination', a war of one race against another.

The Nazis thought the Slav people, such as the Russians, were sub-human, inferior. The Slavs were shown no mercy. They had to make way for *Lebensraum* 'living space' for the Germans. The Nazis believed the Germans were the 'master race'.

When the Germans invaded Russia, some people among the minority groups, like the Ukrainians and Bessarabians, helped the Germans because they wanted independence from the Communists. Most national groups, however, united to fight the Germans. Today the Russians call the war the Great Patriotic War. In areas the Germans captured, *partisans* (resistance fighters) attacked German soldiers and supply lines. If the Germans caught them they were executed (**B**).

The Nazi crimes against the people were many. Special duty groups, *Einsatzgruppen*, followed the fighting troops as they advanced into Russia in 1941. These men were professional mass murderers. Their job was to hunt down and kill all Jews and Communist Party officials.

A German building engineer described the murder of 5000 Jews from one town:

❝ *Men, women and children of all ages had to undress upon the order of an SS man, who carried a dog whip . . . Without screaming or weeping these people undressed, stood around in family groups, kissed each other, said farewells . . . A father*

B The execution of two Russian resistance fighters

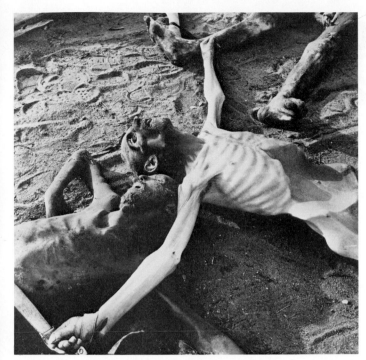

D Millions of Russians died in Nazi camps

was holding the hand of a boy of about 10 years old, the father pointed to the sky, stroked the boy's head and seemed to explain something to him . . .

I found myself faced by a tremendous grave. People were closely wedged together and lying on top of each other so that only their heads were visible. Nearly all had blood running over their shoulders from their heads. Some of the people were still moving. Some were lifting their arms and turning their heads to show that they were still alive . . . I estimated that the pit contained about a thousand people. I looked for the man who did the shooting. He was an SS man, who sat at the edge of the pit, his feet dangling into the pit. He had a tommy gun on his knees and was smoking a cigarette. ❜ (C)

In just two days in 1941 33 771 Jews from Kiev were murdered. Nearly three million people were sent to Germany to work as slave labour. Most died of hunger (D). One German soldier saw the danger of such actions and told his wife:

❛ We behaved like devils out of hell. We left villages to starve to death behind us, thousands and thousands of them. How can you win a war in this way? Do you think they won't revenge themselves somehow? Of course they will. ❜ (E)

Russia suffered more than any other country in the war. Between 20 and 25 million Russians – soldiers and civilians – died. Several million of these died in German labour camps. In 1945 some Russians took their revenge. One German officer wrote:

❛ I saw a whole line of refugees had been rolled over by Russian tanks . . . civilians, mostly women and children, had been squashed flat by the tanks . . . a baby of only a few months, killed by a shot at close range through the forehead. At least one man was nailed to a barn door. ❜ (F)

Stalin's own secret police transported entire national groups, such as the Crimean Tartars. They were sent from Western Russia to remote parts of the USSR. Stalin did not trust such national groups, and feared they might join the Germans. He was also taking the opportunity to remove groups who might cause trouble in the future. Many of these different nationalities died, perhaps up to half a million people.

By 1945 much of Western Russia was in ruins. The war had destroyed or badly damaged over 1700 towns, 70 000 villages, six million houses and nearly 100 000 collective farms. A visitor to Russia wrote:

❛ For thousands of miles there was not a standing or living object to be seen. Every town was flat, every city. There were no barns, no machinery, no stations. There was not a single telegraph pole left standing . . . The houses all being gone, the people were living in dug-outs; pits dug into the earth, and roofed over with fir branches, wattle and earth . . . millions lived like this, not only all over the countryside but also amid the ruins of the great cities. ❜ (G)

It is no wonder that Soviet Russia is determined this will never happen again.

??????????????????

1 Why were the Germans much more cruel towards the Russians than towards the Western Allies?

2 a How did the writer of **E** behave in Russia?
b Why do you think he behaved in this way?
c What do you think he felt about his behaviour when he wrote **E**?

3 a Which pieces of evidence **A–G** are *primary* sources?
b Which ones are *secondary* sources?
c How useful is **A** as evidence for the historian?
d How might **C** help the historian to be more certain about what is said in **A**?

4 a How might a Russian school pupil of your age feel about photograph **B**?
b Do you think the Russians had any excuse for behaving as they did in **F**?

5 How was Russia affected by the war? (Mention: loss of life; damage to industry, towns, the countryside.) What do you think was the worst damage?

25 Decision Making: Teheran, Yalta and Potsdam

As we have seen, one of the main aims of a country's foreign policy is to defend itself against invasion. In 1943 it became clear that the Allies were going to win the war. How was Stalin to prevent future major attacks on Russia, like those of 1914 and 1941? He had to make sure that the countries on Russia's western borders were friendly, and that Germany was never again strong enough to attack Russia.

Decision maker

This section helps you understand Stalin's ideas about what should be done with Eastern Europe after World War II. You must put yourself in the shoes of an adviser to Stalin.

First, look at Points 1–5 below. These show the problem of Eastern Europe, as Stalin saw it.

1 Your first aim is to protect the Soviet Union from invasion.

2 You still fear that if Germany is rebuilt it will pose a major threat to Russia in the future.

3 You also fear the capitalist powers, led by the USA. The USA now has the atomic bomb.

4 Russia is the leader of the Communist world and wants to spread Communism to other countries.

5 You have one great advantage – the Red Army, the largest army in the world, controls most of Eastern Europe.

Now look at the list of **Decisions**. As an adviser, what will you suggest Stalin should do? For each decision, 1–7, write down your choice, and the reasons for it.

The 'Big Three' Allied leaders – Stalin, Churchill and Roosevelt – each had different views on how to treat Germany, and what to do with Poland and other Eastern European countries. The Allies began to try and sort out the future of Europe at three conferences.

Decisions

Decision 1   Will you put on trial the Nazi leaders still alive? What crimes will you charge them with? What will you do with those found guilty?

Decision 2   Will you make Germany pay for the damage done to the Soviet Union? If you make her pay how will you do it:
a take all the machinery and goods you can back to the Soviet Union;
b let her recover first and then pay you?

Decision 3   How will you make sure Germany is never able to attack the Soviet Union again? Choose one option:
a set up a Communist government to run the part of Germany the Red Army controls and make sure this government does as you tell it;
b withdraw the Red Army and allow Germans to elect the government they want;
c make Germany a pastoral country (a country based on farming) with no important industry;
d work out your own proposal involving the new world organisation: the United Nations.

Decision 4   How will you make sure Poland, which shares a long border with you, will always be an ally? It separates you from the Germans who have twice come through Poland to attack you. Choose one or two options:
a take a strip of Poland's land along your border and give Poland a strip of Germany's land;

b set up a Communist government friendly to the Soviet Union;
c withdraw the Red Army and allow Poles to elect the government they want.

Decision 5   How will you make sure Rumania, which also shares a long border with you, will remain an ally? Choose one or two options:
a take a strip of Rumania's land along your border;
b withdraw the Red Army and allow Rumanians to elect the government they want;
c set up a Communist government friendly to the Soviet Union.

Decision 6   What will you do with the other countries in eastern Europe: Czechoslovakia, Hungary, Bulgaria, Yugoslavia and Greece? Will you:
a try to set up Communist governments friendly to the Soviet Union;
b allow them to elect the governments they want?

Decision 7   What will you do about the Baltic countries: Lithuania, Estonia and Latvia? Choose one option:
a make them part of Russia, which they were before 1917;
b set up Communist governments friendly to the Soviet Union;
c let them remain independent and elect the governments they want?

The first meeting was at Teheran in Iran in 1943 when the Red Army was pushing back the Germans. The 'Big Three' made clear that they had only one aim at this time, the destruction of Germany and Japan.

In February 1945, with the war almost won, Stalin, Churchill and Roosevelt met again at Yalta in the USSR. Differences between Stalin and his allies were growing, but were as yet still hidden by the common aim of beating Germany. The Allies agreed:

'*to destroy Nazism . . . to disarm and disband all German forces . . . to remove and destroy all German military equipment . . . to bring all war criminals to just and swift punishment and to take reparations* (payments for war damage).' (A)

The last meeting was in July 1945 at Potsdam after Germany had surrendered. Clement Attlee, the new British Prime Minister, took Churchill's place, while Harry Truman was the new American President, Roosevelt having died. B shows what was agreed at Teheran, Yalta and Potsdam.

B Results of the peace conferences in 1944/45

TEHERAN November 1943 (Stalin, Churchill, Roosevelt)
a Britain and America to open a 'Second Front' in France early in 1944.
b After the war Russia would gain part of Poland and Poland would gain part of Germany.
c Russia to enter the war against Japan when Germany was defeated.
d Agreed on the idea of a new world organisation to replace the League of Nations.

YALTA February 1945 (Stalin, Churchill, Roosevelt)
e Germany to be divided into four zones (Russian, British, American, French). Berlin also to be divided.
f Russia to enter the war against Japan three months after the defeat of Germany.
g Further agreement on a world organisation to keep the peace.
h Bessarabia and the Baltic States of Lithuania, Latvia and Estonia to become part of the USSR.
i Russia to have most influence in Rumania, Bulgaria, Hungary and Poland, but will allow some non-Communists in the governments of these countries.

POTSDAM July 1945 (Stalin, Truman, Churchill/Attlee)
j For the time being, Germany to be run by a Control Council made up of the four military commanders of the four zones.
k Elections to be held in Germany some time in the the future.
l Nazi leaders to be put on trial at Nuremberg for causing the war and for crimes against the human race.
m Reparations: each power to take what it wanted from its own zone. The Soviet Union could also take 25% of the industrial equipment in the other zones.
n Similar arrangements made for Austria.

Map C shows how Germany emerged from the conferences. Potsdam marked the end of the wartime alliance between the USSR, Britain and the USA. The three conferences left plenty of things undecided. What was to happen to Germany in the long run had not been agreed, so it stayed divided. Stalin's mistrust of the Western powers grew. He soon began to feel that the only way to make sure the governments of the Eastern European countries were friendly was to ensure they were Communist. For their part, Britain and the USA wanted to stop the spread of Communism.

Look back at your list of *Decisions*. How good were you as an adviser? How many of your decisions were actually taken at the peace conferences?

C The zones of Germany and frontier changes by 1946

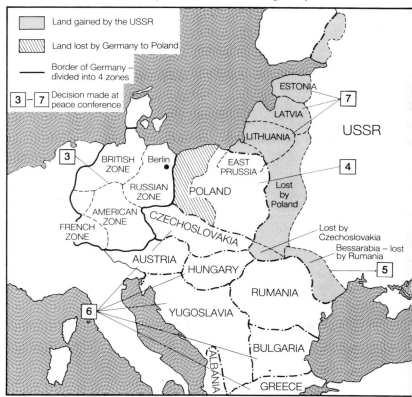

??????????????????

1 a Who were the 'Big Three'?
b What lands did the USSR eventually gain (see **B** and **C**)?

2 a What type of governments do the countries in decision **i** at Yalta (**B**) have today?
b What did decisions **j** and **k** at Potsdam leave unsettled? Why do you think this was important?

3 In pairs or small groups, discuss Decisions **1–7**. Which policies would you recommend Stalin to follow at Potsdam in 1945? Give reasons for your choices.

26 The Soviet Empire in Europe

Between 1945 and 1949 Stalin created a Russian empire in Eastern Europe. This empire included Poland, Hungary, Rumania, Bulgaria, Czechoslovakia and East Germany. Each had a Communist government. In the West we usually speak of these countries as 'satellite states' because they cling closely to the Soviet Union like satellites round a planet.

Stalin built the empire in stages (**A**).

It was a matter of getting Communists into the new governments and getting other people out – and keeping them out. This pattern of events was more or less the same in each 'satellite' country (see map **B**).

In Yugoslavia it was different. Josip Tito, the Communist leader and a war hero, was more independent. He did not want to see his country become a Russian satellite. He refused to obey Stalin's orders and was prepared to trade with non-communist countries. Stalin told the Yugoslavs to overthrow Tito but they ignored this. Then Stalin tried to starve Tito into surrender by ordering Communist countries not to trade with Yugoslavia. This also failed. Yugoslavia remained outside the 'satellite empire' of the Soviet Union. Tito made his reasons clear:

> ‹*This conflict arose from the purely aggressive policy of the USSR towards Yugoslavia, from attempts to enslave our country economically and politically, to remove its independence and to make it into a colony.*› (**C**)

Tito was correct. Stalin demanded that his satellites must obey him. They had to help defend the Soviet Union and serve the Soviet economy, wrecked after four years of war.

In 1947 the Americans threatened Stalin's plans when President Truman warned that America would support any country wishing to stop any other country from running its affairs. Truman meant the Communist countries under pressure from Stalin to obey him. Truman's message is called the *Truman Doctrine*. Part of the Truman Doctrine was the *Marshall Plan*. Under the Marshall Plan the USA gave huge amounts of money and aid to help countries build up their industry, trade and farming after the war.

A How Stalin created Russian 'satellites'

Stage 1 Communists from these countries were trained in Moscow before the war.

Stage 2 Many of them were included in the new governments set up in 1945. This was not difficult as the elections of 1945 created coalition governments made up of parties who had opposed the Nazis.

Stage 3 The Communists were given many of the important jobs such as control of the police, broadcasting and army. This helped in the next stage.

Stage 4 Non-Communists were removed from power, this was often done by accusing them of treason or corruption, or by using violence.

Stage 5 All other political parties were banned.

B The Soviet Empire in Europe

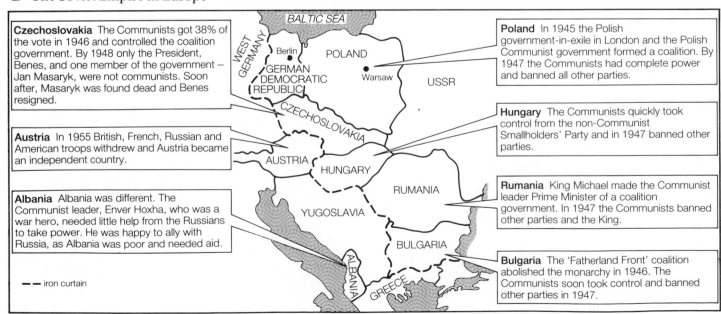

Czechoslovakia The Communists got 38% of the vote in 1946 and controlled the coalition government. By 1948 only the President, Benes, and one member of the government – Jan Masaryk, were not communists. Soon after, Masaryk was found dead and Benes resigned.

Austria In 1955 British, French, Russian and American troops withdrew and Austria became an independent country.

Albania Albania was different. The Communist leader, Enver Hoxha, who was a war hero, needed little help from the Russians to take power. He was happy to ally with Russia, as Albania was poor and needed aid.

Poland In 1945 the Polish government-in-exile in London and the Polish Communist government formed a coalition. By 1947 the Communists had complete power and banned all other parties.

Hungary The Communists quickly took control from the non-Communist Smallholders' Party and in 1947 banned other parties.

Rumania King Michael made the Communist leader Prime Minister of a coalition government. In 1947 the Communists banned other parties and the King.

Bulgaria The 'Fatherland Front' coalition abolished the monarchy in 1946. The Communists soon took control and banned other parties in 1947.

– – – iron curtain

1946

March   In a speech Churchill attacks Russia. He says an 'iron curtain' divides the Russian-controlled area of Europe from Western Europe, and accuses Stalin of crushing freedom.
Poland Pro-Communist National Front coalition party wins 90% of the vote and forms a communist government.
Greece Civil war in Greece between communists and backers of Britain. Stalin refuses to help the communists, despite their backing from communist governments of Albania, Bulgaria and Yugoslavia.

1947

         Poland Opposition to communists ends. Opponents of communists flee to the West.
March   Truman plan announced.
June   Marshall Aid announced.
October Bulgaria, Hungary, Poland, Rumania now fully communist and under Russian control. *Cominform* set up to give Moscow full control over these countries. Under ex-resistance leader Tito, Yugoslavia, a communist country free of Russian control, begins to quarrel with Stalin.

1948

March   Communists seize power in Czechoslovakia, and murder or drive out their enemies.
May   Election confirms communists as only party in Czechoslovakia. Russia has now set up communist parties in all the countries her army occupied in 1945.
June   Tito's Yugoslavia thrown out of Cominform. Russians begin Berlin Blockade.

1949

April   NATO (North Atlantic Treaty Organisation) set up as anti-Russian military alliance of West European powers.
May   End of Berlin Blockade.

Stalin feared this help would weaken his control over the satellite countries. He would not allow them to accept it. To help control his satellites Stalin set up *Cominform* (the Communist Information Bureau) in 1947. It was really a new version of *Comintern* (see page 43). This was Stalin's answer to the Truman Doctrine.

His answer to Marshall Aid was *Comecon* (Council of Mutual Economic Aid). This was set up in 1949 and Stalin used it to link the economies of his satellites to that of the Soviet Union. Each satellite produced what Stalin wanted it to. Poland, for example, concentrated on coal and steel.

Germany, however, was still a problem (see pages 50–51). The Russians had stripped their zone of anything of value. This angered the Western Allies, who felt that Europe could not recover from the war unless Germany also recovered. In 1948 the British, French and American zones united to form a 'Tri-zone' for economic purposes and introduced a new currency. The Americans declared:

'*We shall do everything in our power to secure the maximum possible unification . . . Germany is a part of Europe and recovery in Europe . . . will be slow indeed if Germany with all her great resources of coal and iron is turned into a poorhouse.*' (**D**)

Stalin feared the 'rebirth' of Germany and the power of the West. He acted quickly and imposed a *blockade* on Berlin. This meant cutting all road, rail and canal routes between the Western zones and West Berlin (across the Russian zone). Stalin hoped to starve the Western powers out. But the Allies flew in supplies, and in May 1949 the blockade was lifted. In September the three Western zones formed an independent state, the Federal Republic of Germany. In October the Russian zone became the German Democratic Republic.

The crisis over Berlin increased the distrust and hostility between Russia and the USA. A state of Cold War existed. This was a war of words and trade rivalry, which stopped short of actual fighting. By 1950 Stalin had full control over the Communist governments of Eastern Europe, which the Russians had set up (see **E**). Winston Churchill's 'iron curtain' seemed to have become a reality.

??????????????

1 Explain the terms: satellite state; Truman Doctrine; Marshall Aid; Cominform; Comecon.

2 **a** Why did Tito resist Stalin (**C**)?
b Write a report for a Russian newspaper attacking Tito's speech (**C**) and giving the Russian view of Stalin's 'satellite' policy.

3 Using the evidence in this section, draw up a chart to explain why and how Russia took over Eastern Europe from 1945–48 and how America reacted.

RUSSIA		AMERICA	
action	*reason*	*action*	*reason*
1946–7 Communist Party gains power in Eastern Europe	need for buffer zones	Truman doctrine	fear of Communist takeover

27 Khrushchev's Russia

In his last years Stalin began to see enemies all around him. The purges returned and the Soviet Union became closed off to the outside world. Stalin was worried about the future. He warned the Party leaders:

‹ You are blind like young kittens, what will happen without me? The country will perish because you are unable to recognise our enemies . . . You'll see, when I'm gone the imperialistic powers will wring your necks like chickens. › **(A)**

On 5 March 1953 Moscow radio announced Stalin's death. Stalin had ruthlessly forced the Soviet people to build the first Communist state and make it the world's second superpower. Who would take control now?

The Party leaders announced there would be a collective leadership – no more one-man rule. By 1955, however, Nikita Khrushchev had emerged to dominate the collective leaderships. But he was never to become a dictator like Stalin.

Khrushchev, like Stalin, came from a peasant family. He tells us:

C Khrushchev on an official visit to Tselinny Territory – receiving the traditional gifts of bread and salt

‹ My grandfather was a serf, the property of a landlord who could sell him if he wished or trade him for a hunting dog . . . I began working as soon as I could walk. (In the coal mines, aged 15.) › **(B)**

Stalin had been a remote, god-like figure but Khrushchev saw himself as a man of the people (see C). He even met and shook hands with ordinary people. The purges ended and there was more freedom. This was a big change from Stalin's rule. The people had been taught that Stalin was always right. Khrushchev had to destroy this myth. In 1956 at the Twentieth Communist Party Congress he condemned Stalin for being a dictator and for building up a 'personality cult'. It was wrong, said Khrushchev:

‹ to elevate one person, to transform him into a superman with supernatural characteristics like those of a god. Such a man supposedly knows everything, sees everything, thinks for everyone, is never wrong in his behaviour . . . Stalin discarded Lenin's methods of convincing and education . . . for those of violence, mass repressions and terror. Confessions of guilt were gained with the help of cruel and inhuman tortures. › **(D)**

Suddenly the leader who had never been wrong was under attack. This came as a great shock to most Russians. Although Khrushchev's speech was never made public (it was called the 'secret speech'), Russians soon knew about it. Khrushchev's policy, 'de-Stalinisation', meant the removal of portraits and statues of Stalin. Stalingrad was even renamed Volgagrad.

Most people welcomed the speech, but some thought Khrushchev had gone too far. In 1957 some Party

E Khrushchev's agricultural reforms

The *aim* was to increase food production:

1 Food prices were raised to encourage production.
2 Collective farms were given greater freedom to run themselves.
3 Money was invested in farm machinery and fertilizers.
4 Peasants could sell produce from private plots more easily.
5 Motor Tractor Stations were abolished. The machinery was sold to the collective farms.
6 Very large areas of unused or 'virgin' land in Siberia and Kazakhstan were ploughed and sown in the Virgin Lands scheme. In 1954 more than the total cultivated land in England, France and Spain was ploughed up.

Result: Food production increased but not to the amount promised. The Virgin Lands scheme had two good harvests but then over-cultivation led to soil erosion and harvests failed. Collective farms were still inefficient.

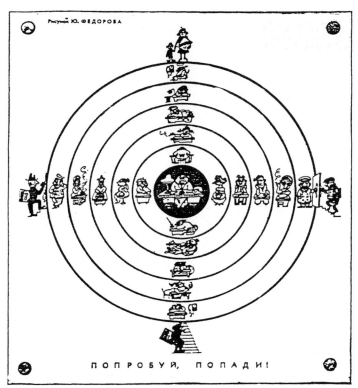

ПОПРОБУЙ, ПОПАДИ!

F This 1965 cartoon criticises *over-centralisation*. Everyone depends on the man at the centre. The woman at the top has a declaration, the man on the left has a complaint, the woman at the bottom wants help, the man on the right has a petition . . .

leaders tried to remove him but failed. Khrushchev continued to try and reform Stalin's system of running Russia. He was determined to improve the standard of living. This meant improving agriculture (see **E**) and industry. The main problem was over-centralisation (**F**), nothing could be done without permission from an official in Moscow and a lot of paperwork. Khrushchev began a policy of *decentralisation*. Managers of farms and factories could make more decisions. Major planning decisions were made by regional councils. The large planning ministries in Moscow were closed.

A Five Year Plan started in 1956 but was replaced by a Seven Year Plan in 1959. The main aim was still the growth of heavy industry, but more consumer goods were also made. In 1961 Khrushchev boasted:

❝ *At present the USSR has already outstripped the United States in iron ore, coal, coke, prefabricated concrete elements, heavy diesel and electric locomotives, sawn timber, woollen textiles, sugar, butter, fish . . . little more time will be required to outstrip the United States economically.* ❞ (**G**)

Although output increased (**H**), the regional councils did not work well and muddle and inefficiency continued.

The Russian standard of living improved a great deal between 1953 and 1964. There were still shortages but

H Economic development 1954–64

	1954	1964
Steel	42 million tonnes	85 million tonnes
Crude oil	59 million tonnes	224 million tonnes
Woollen cloth	159 000 tonnes	239 000 tonnes
Wheat	42 million tonnes	74 million tonnes
Cattle	57 million	85 million
Radios and televisions	3 154 000	4 766 000
Cars	95 000	185 000

wages rose faster than prices and more kinds of goods could be bought. Many new flats were built and there were pensions and free education. Soviet citizens were very proud of achievements such as the first artificial satellite, *Sputnik I*, launched in 1957, and the first manned spaceflight by Yuri Gagarin in 1961.

Despite these successes many of Khrushchev's reforms failed. This lost him some support, but it was probably his failures in foreign policy which led to his downfall in 1964.

The Soviet Empire

Look back at the map on page 52. Which countries were satellites of the Soviet Empire? Soon after Stalin's death in 1953 Soviet tanks had to crush a workers' revolt in East Berlin. Even so, Khrushchev relaxed Soviet control over the satellites as part of his de-Stalinisation policy. Stalin's supporters were dismissed from the satellite governments and more personal freedom was allowed. In 1955 Khrushchev even tried to improve relations with Yugoslavia by visiting Marshal Tito. Soviet Russia, however, could not forget the war and the danger of an enemy gaining control of Eastern Europe. Khrushchev would not let the satellites break free from Soviet domination. In 1955 Khrushchev and the satellite states signed the Warsaw Pact, a military alliance. But in 1956 two major problems arose. The trouble began in Poland. Strikes and demonstrations demanding less Soviet control forced Khrushchev to agree to the popular communist war hero, Wladyslaw Gomulka, becoming leader.

In Hungary workers and students, encouraged by events in Poland, demanded even more drastic changes. They succeeded in making the moderate Communist Imre Nagy, Prime Minister. Nagy ordered Soviet forces to leave. Instead, when Nagy said Hungary would withdraw from the Warsaw Pact, the Red Army attacked Budapest (**J**).

After fierce fighting the Hungarians were defeated, 3000 died and Nagy was executed. Khrushchev explained:

Daily Mirror
RED ARMY TANKS POUR IN

SAT OCT 27 1956

2ᴰ FORWARD WITH THE PEOPLE
No. 16,447

One street in Budapest—a line of Soviet tanks, their guns at the ready, are on patrol.

J Headlines from the *Daily Mirror*, 27 October 1956

'*We certainly had no intention of doing what the leader of a revolt told us to do . . . The working class refused to support Nagy . . . In Budapest the people put up rather stubborn resistance.*' (**K**)

While de-Stalinisation was welcomed by the Poles and Hungarians it shocked some Communists, especially the Chinese and Albanians, who continued to support the ideas of Stalin.

Outside the Soviet Empire

After 1953 the 'Cold War' was changing. The Soviet Union had tested its first atom bomb in 1949 and the more powerful hydrogen bomb in 1953. The nuclear arms race with America was hotting up. Khrushchev understood the threat, and he changed Soviet foreign policy. Instead of claiming that conflict with capitalist countries was certain, he adopted a policy of 'peaceful co-existence'. Peaceful co-existence meant peaceful competition and even co-operation with the West.

But peaceful co-existence turned out to vary from friendly relations at one moment to hostility on the brink of war the next. Khrushchev was prepared to co-operate with the West, but he was ready to threaten to use force if he thought it would work. **L** shows the main events in the Cold War up to 1954.

In October 1964 the Politburo asked Khrushchev to retire 'in view of his health and age'. Khrushchev had made too many mistakes. The Cuban failure (see **L**) meant he was thought to be too soft towards the West. Also, he had failed to solve Russia's economic problem.

L The Cold War 1955–63

	Event	Outcome
1955	Summit Conference at Geneva between the leaders of the USSR, USA, Britain and France.	A friendly meeting but no real progress on disarmament and Berlin.
1956	Khrushchev visited Britain.	Visits well received in both countries.
1959	Khrushchev visited the USA.	
1960	Summit Conference at Paris.	Khrushchev walked out in anger because the Americans refused to apologise for the American U2 spy plane shot down over Russia.
1961	The Berlin Wall, separating East and West Berlin, was built to stop East Germans leaving via West Berlin.	This closed the last gap in the iron curtain and although the West protested it made Berlin a less dangerous problem.
1962	Khrushchev met US President Kennedy at Vienna.	Failed to agree to end arms race.
1962	Cuban missile crisis: Kennedy forced Khrushchev to dismantle missile sites being built in Cuba by blockading the island.	The world came close to nuclear war. The teleprinter 'hot-line' between the two leaders was set up. Khrushchev's colleagues saw the crisis as a setback.
1963	Nuclear Test Ban Treaty signed with the USA and Britain.	Restricted testing of nuclear weapons.

??????????????????

1 Explain the terms: collective leadership; de-Stalinisation; over-centralisation; Virgin lands scheme; peaceful co-existence.

2 How successful was Khrushchev? Look at the evidence beside each point below. With a partner, work out your ideas on how successful the evidence shows Khrushchev to be, and write them down.

	Evidence
De-Stalinisation	A, C, D, F
Agricultural reform	E, G, H
Industrial output	G, H
The Soviet empire	J, K
Foreign policy	L

Now use your notes, the evidence, and anything else you can find, to answer the question 'Was Khrushchev a failure or a success? Discuss'.

28 Relations with China

Stalin had given little help to Mao Zedong and the Chinese Communists in their struggle for power. Despite this, the two countries signed a Treaty of Friendship in 1950. Stalin gave economic aid and sent Soviet scientists and technicians to help build up Chinese industry.

Under Khrushchev things began well. He visited China in 1954 and sent more aid. But his de-Stalinisation policy shocked Mao, who saw it as an attack on his own style of leadership. Khrushchev later wrote:

❝ *Clearly, there was a fairly basic disagreement between us. But it went deeper. Stalin was exposed and condemned for having had hundreds of thousands of people shot and for his abuse of power. Mao Zedong was following in Stalin's footsteps.* ❞ (A)

Also, Mao disagreed with Khrushchev's idea of 'peaceful co-existence' with Western countries. Mao thought this was betraying the ideas of Marx and Lenin, by not encouraging Communist revolution in other countries, and said Khrushchev was guilty of 'Revisionism'. Khrushchev argued that Mao did not understand the danger of nuclear war and the threat from the USA. Khrushchev called Mao's policy 'Adventurism'.

In 1960 Khrushchev ended Soviet aid to China. He withdrew Russian advisors and technicians, leaving some factories half-built. Rivalry built up between the USSR and China, with each side insulting the other.

A major cause of trouble was the long border between the two countries (see **B**). In the nineteenth century China had been forced to give territory to Russia. Now Mao wanted it back. Along the border, Soviet and Chinese troops showed their dislike of one another, as Norman Barrymaine, a British journalist remembered:

❝ *Another favourite habit* (of the Chinese) *was forming up on the river ice, sticking tongues out in unison at the Soviet troops, then turning and dropping trousers to the Russians in an ancient gesture of contempt.* ❞ (C)

Arguments and disputes continued. Then, in 1969, serious fighting broke out on the border, along the Ussuri and Amur rivers (see **B**). Each side blamed the other. The Russians said:

❝ *The armed provocation staged by the Chinese was planned in advance . . . On 12 August Soviet frontier guards saw army units being moved up on the Chinese side of this section of the frontier.* ❞ (D)

The Chinese version was that

❝ *. . . large numbers of fully armed Soviet soldiers, together with armoured vehicles intruded into Chinese territory . . . outrageously opened up with cannon and gun fire on the Chinese frontier guards who were forced to fight back in self-defence.* ❞ (E)

Relations did not improve in the 1970s. The Chinese objected to Soviet involvement in Vietnam and to the invasion of Afghanistan in 1979. Today, Soviet leaders are aware that China has built up a stock of nuclear arms, uncomfortably close to the Soviet border.

B The Russian/Chinese border

- - - - Border
///// Territory claimed by USSR
▓▓▓▓ Territory claimed by China

USSR

MONGOLIA

MANCHURIA

Amur

Ussuri

Vladivostok

CHINA

500   1000 km

??????????????????

1 a What did Khrushchev mean in **A** when he said that Mao 'was following in Stalin's footsteps'?
b Why did Mao disagree with 'peaceful co-operation'?
c How did Chinese troops taunt the Russians (**C**)?

2 Look at **D** and **E**.
a What do the words: provocation; intruded; outrageously; mean?
b What do these words tell you about the attitude of each side?
c What extra information does **E** give you that **D** does not?
d How reliable do you think these statements are as evidence about the fighting? Why?

3 Explain why Soviet Russia's relations with China have been uneasy since 1949.

29 The USSR since 1964

After Khrushchev 'retired', three new leaders came to power. They were Leonid Brezhnev, Alexei Kosygin and Nikolai Podgorny (A). Brezhnev was the leading figure. He was the new General Secretary of the Communist Party, and he soon came to control the Politburo.

1964. The new Soviet leaders face the same problems as Khrushchev. The Soviet economy is like a large, creaking machine. Lots of planners decide what to do. The economy swallows massive amounts of money, but it is inefficient compared with that of the West. *Productivity* (output per worker) is low.

The Politburo draws up Five Year Plans and annual targets for each industry. The planners set output figures for each factory. Many factory managers are not keen to produce more, in case their targets are put up next year. Often workers take it easy at the start of the month, then rush at the end to meet the monthly target. This is known as 'storming the target' and can result in poor quality goods. Soviet shoppers often refuse to buy goods if the date stamp shows they were made after the 18th of the month.

Other problems which affect production include alcoholism, absenteeism, stealing and corruption. Many goods are in short supply. People are used to long queues. All this leads to a thriving 'underground economy' as one American visitor discovered in 1976:

Russian friends tipped me off that it was not money that really mattered, but access or 'blat' (influence or knowing the right people) *. . . almost everyone can give the benefits of blat to someone else — a doorman, a cleaning lady in a food store, a sales clerk, a car mechanic or a professor — because each has access to things or services that are hard to get.* (B)

Brezhnev had to decide how much money to invest in the economy, in particular industry, agriculture and defence. Industry and defence had always received most. Brezhnev wanted to increase production but also improve living standards by making better food and consumer goods.

Several ways were tried. First Kosygin gave managers more freedom to make decisions. Some factories received bonuses for goods sold, rather than the amount made. This scheme ended in 1970. It had not been a success. Brezhnev appealed to people's patriotism to make them work harder. The Five Year Plan of 1971–76 promised more consumer goods. Brezhnev said things were changing:

The long years of heroic history when millions of Communists and non-Party people deliberately made sacrifices and underwent hardship . . . are behind us . . . it is unacceptable under present conditions. (C)

Further changes in 1973 and 1979 failed to solve the major problems: poor quality and low productivity. But the standard of living did improve. More consumer goods were available (see D). More meat, milk and vegetables meant a more varied diet. A British newspaper correspondent living in Moscow had already noted, in 1967:

This winter it has usually been possible to get oranges, apples and even bananas in quite ordinary shops outside the city

A From left to right: Nikolai Podgorny, Leonid Brezhnev, Alexei Kosygin

D Consumer goods in the USSR

	1955	1966	1980
	(No. per thousand of population)	(No. per thousand of population)	(No. per thousand of families)
Radios	66	171	850
Cars	2	5	90
TV sets	4	82	830
Washing machines	1	77	700
Refrigerators	4	40	860

centre. This was not so two years ago. The young people are noticeably better dressed. **9 (E)**

In the countryside wages and living standards improved. Economic growth, however, slowed down in the 1970s and '80s. To help the economy grow, the USSR was keen to use more advanced Western technology. Western companies built car and chemical plants and developed oil fields in the USSR.

Agriculture continued to be the weak link in the Soviet economy. Collectivised agriculture is inefficient. Peasants tended to give most care and attention to their small private plots. These plots made up only 1 per cent of cultivated land, but they produced a staggering 25 per cent of farm output. To increase the size of private plots would not, however, fit in with Communist beliefs.

Brezhnev invested more in machinery and fertilizers and increased the amount paid to peasants for their products. Agricultural production increased slowly (see

F Grain harvests 1953–79 (millions of tonnes)

1953	1956	1959	1962	1965	1968	1971	1974	1977	1978	1979
83	125	120	140	121	170	181	195	196	235	179

G The Russian *Salyut* space station under construction

F) but there were still major problems. Many skilled peasants preferred to find work in the towns, leaving the older, unskilled peasants on the farms. Also, the climate and soil in many of the new farming areas was not suited to agriculture. In most years the USSR imported large amounts of grain, paying for it by exporting oil and natural gas.

One of Soviet Russia's successes has been its space programme. In 1965 the first person to walk in space was a Russian. Huge *Salyut* space stations (**G**) were sent into orbit in the early 1980s, enabling cosmonauts to stay in space for months.

Brezhnev died in November 1982. Although he never had the personal power of Stalin or Khrushchev, he was praised as a great leader in speeches and newspapers. On his seventieth birthday a supporter in the Politburo had said:

(*The Party and people love you, Leonid. They love you for your humanity and warmth, for your wisdom and endless devotion to Leninism.* **9 (H)**

Yuri Andropov, head of the KGB, became the new leader. He began to attack corruption in the Party and the government, but in February 1984 he died. Next came Konstantin Chernenko, but he too died in 1985. A younger man, Mikhail Gorbachev, became the new leader.

??????????????

1 Explain the meaning of: storming the target; underground economy; private plots.

2 a What ideas about the Russian leaders do you think the official photograph, **A**, is trying to get across?
b What did Brezhnev mean in **C** by 'the long years of sacrifice and hardship'?

3 a What new goods became available in the shops in 1980 according to **D**? How might Russians have got hold of them before?
b What does the presence of these goods suggest about the Russian economy in the 1980s? Does other evidence on these pages support or contradict this?

4 Look at **D** and **F**. What other evidence might you need in order to judge how well the Soviet economy did from 1955–80?

5 How does your life compare with that of a Russian student of your own age? (Use newspapers, magazines, television and radio programmes and any other information you can find to help you.)

30 Soviet Foreign Policy since 1964

Your teacher may not agree with all you read in this section. People interpret the evidence about Soviet foreign policy differently, so sometimes they disagree. Many people believe Soviet Russia is trying to take over the world, others believe America is trying to do this. Some people ignore the evidence altogether! Remember that Soviet leaders do not trust the West. Remember also the 20 million Soviet people killed in the war and the importance of the East European states to Soviet defence.

Détente

Khrushchev's policy of peaceful co-existence was continued by Brezhnev and Kosygin. It developed into *détente* (a French word which means to relax or slacken tension, as two tug-of-war teams might slacken tension on the rope). The word détente is used to describe the improvement in relations between East and West from 1964 to the late 1970s.

After 1964 Soviet leaders increasingly feared American economic and military strength and were very worried about the defence of Russia. Jonathan Steele, a British journalist and expert on East European affairs, explained that the Soviet leaders had:

❛*a desire for docile buffer states or friendly neighbours on their immediate borders, and a fear of encirclement* (being surrounded). *World communist revolution is something that they do not expect to see in their lifetime, or would unreservedly welcome.*❜ **(A)**

(Jonathan Steele, *World Power* 1983)

Fear of encirclement (see map **B**) and American superiority may well have made Brezhnev anxious to avoid conflict, and led him to support détente. Détente and the enormous cost of the Arms Race led eventually to the Strategic Arms Limitation Treaty (SALT 1) in 1972. The Soviet newspaper *Pravda* said:

❛(SALT) *must promote the checking of the arms drive which creates the threat of a rocket-nuclear conflict, and diverts vast resources from more creative tasks.*❜ **(C)**

Eastern Europe

The Russians see control of Eastern Europe as vital to the defence of the USSR. In 1968 they were alarmed when the Czech leader, Alexander Dubcek, introduced reforms allowing free political parties and trade unions. Brezhnev feared Czechoslovakia might break away and so weaken the Warsaw Pact.

On 20 August Warsaw Pact forces invaded Czechos-

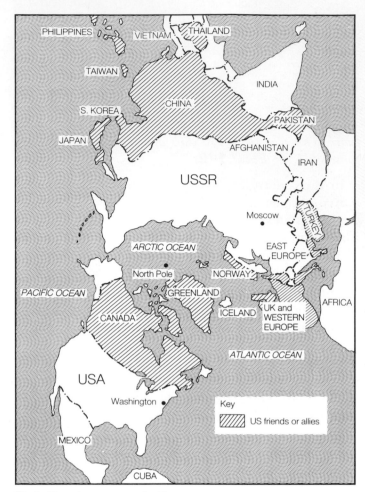

B Is Russia surrounded?

Key
⧄ US friends or allies

lovakia. The Czechs were hostile but there was little fighting. The Soviets removed Dubcek from office. The West condemned the invasion but Brezhnev argued that he had the right to intervene to protect the Warsaw Pact:

❛*When internal and external forces hostile to Socialism attempt to turn the development of any Socialist country in the direction of the capitalist system . . . when a threat arises to the . . . security of the Socialist commonwealth as a whole — it becomes not only a problem for the people of that country but also a general problem, the concern of all Socialist countries.*❜ **(D)**

Another problem came in 1980 in Poland. Workers forced the government to accept the free trade union *Solidarity*, led by Lech Walesa. Solidarity demanded free elections; it appeared Poland might break free of Soviet influence. Brezhnev backed the Polish army and General Jaruzelski, who took control and banned Solidarity.

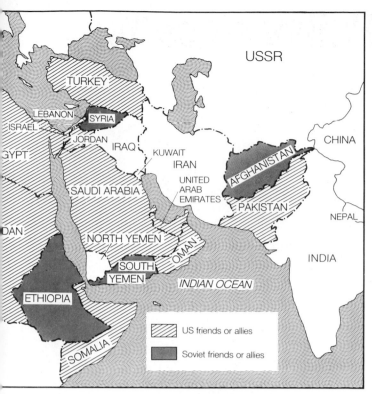

E Russia's relations with the Middle East and West Asia

Legend:
- US friends or allies
- Soviet friends or allies

Outside Europe

Soviet influence in Asia declined after 1964. Russia's main ally was North Vietnam. The Soviets helped the Communist Government in the North in the war against the American-backed Government of the South.

Map **E** shows some of the countries which the Soviet leaders were concerned about. The main problem was China (see page 57). But the leaders were also worried about the growth in Iran of Moslem *fundamentalism* (extreme religious beliefs and a strict, traditional way of life). They feared this might spread to the Moslems in Russia.

In 1979 Soviet troops moved into Afghanistan to support the Communist Government which was about to collapse. Many countries condemned this 'invasion' and détente suffered badly. The Soviets argued:

❝ *Soviet aid to Afghanistan in no way interferes with détente. The Soviet Union responded to a request by the Afghan government, and gave aid to a country that had been the victim of aggression.* ❞ **(F)**

Inside Afghanistan, Soviet troops fought a drawn-out and costly war against the *Mujaheddin*, the Afghan resistance movement.

Elsewhere, Soviet Russia struggled for influence against both America and China. The main weapons were trade agreements and military aid. In general Soviet leaders showed little interest in helping Left Wing groups in countries far from Russia. The exception was Cuba, Russia's main ally in the Caribbean. Otherwise, the USSR did not wish to clash with the USA in South and Central America.

In Africa the USSR has influence in Communist countries like Angola, Ethiopia and Mozambique. But the economies of most African countries are closely tied to the West, and Russia does not have the economic power to change this.

Soviet leaders are more involved in the Middle East where they support the Arabs against the Israelis. The main Soviet allies are Syria and Libya, but Russia has not always found the Arabs the best of allies: in 1976 Egypt threw the Russians out.

The New Cold War

Détente did not survive. In the late 1970s America wanted to use détente to force a change in Soviet foreign policy and improve human rights in Russia. This was unacceptable to the USSR. The two Superpowers, like tug-of-war teams, took up the strain and a new Cold War began. Soviet leaders were concerned by the tough policy of President Reagan, expressed in warnings by the US Government:

❝ *The Soviet Union would have to choose between peacefully changing their Communist system in the direction followed by the West or going to war.* ❞ **(G)**

???????????????

1 a What does *détente* mean?
b How is it used to describe relations between East and West?
c What happened to détente in the late 1970s?

2 a What is *encirclement* (**B**)?
b Why do you think it worries Russia's leaders?

3 As if you were an adviser to US President Reagan, write a report (about 500 words) explaining the main points of Soviet foreign policy. Use the evidence in this section and anything else you can find. Your report will *brief* (prepare) President Reagan for a meeting with the Soviet leader, Mr Gorbachev, in Geneva in November 1985.

31 Opposition

Warning! If you lived in Soviet Russia it would be dangerous for you to read on. You are not allowed to read the books from which **A** and **B** are taken. If you did, this might happen:

'. . . *pushing him* (my father) *aside, four men came into the room, three in civilian clothes and one in a policeman's uniform.*' (**A**)

You could end up in a prison such as this:

'*The cell was cramped . . . the tiny window was barred. No mattresses or bedding were allowed. The bunks were short, you had to sleep bent double. In one corner stood the slop-tank (toilet bucket) . . . it filled the cell with an unspeakable stench.* (Outside) *twenty to thirty degrees of frost. We stamped about the tiny yard, with our hands in our sleeves and our heads lowered. Those who have no strength at all, slump down in the corner . . . slowly freezing.*' (**B**)

How long could you live like this? Anatoly Marchenko, who wrote **B**, was sentenced to six years in prison. His crime was to try to leave the Soviet Union. After his release he criticised the Soviet Government and was sentenced to another four years.

What happens if you criticise the British Government? No one openly cares, although your name might go into a file which our security police, MI5, keep. In the Soviet Union you would not have the same freedom to speak out against the government, nor the right to publish work like **A** and **B**. Some Russians demand more freedom. They are known as *dissidents* (this means someone who disagrees with the government). A few dissidents publish their views in *samizdat*, secretly printed magazines. The KGB, the secret police, keep a constant watch on dissidents, and follow and harass them. The government makes out that the dissidents are traitors, and most Russians disapprove of them.

Dissident protest was strongest in the USSR in the 1960s and '70s. In 1975 Soviet Russia signed the *Helsinki Agreement* promising human rights for everyone, but by the early 1980s most dissidents had been silenced. Some, like the writer Alexander Solzhenitsyn, were deported. Others, like the scientist André Sakharov, were sent into internal exile. Many dissidents are still in prisons, labour camps or 'mental hospitals' (see **C** and **D**). Opposition is not tolerated.

Sometimes the deep national and religious divisions in Soviet society lead to opposition to the government. There are 15 republics in the USSR (see map **E**) and

C A cell in the Troizkoje Psychiatric Clinic – this photograph was taken without official permission and smuggled out of Russia

D Kaschenko Mental Hospital, where some Russian Christians are imprisoned

over 130 different nationalities. The Tsars tried to 'Russify' these non-Russian people: merge them into one people. Stalin and then Khrushchev continued this 'Russification' but Brezhnev more or less stopped it. Some national groups no longer feel threatened but some Estonians and Lithuanians continue to demand greater cultural and economic freedom. For many of these people, being a member of their national group comes before being a Soviet citizen. Some of them want independence. Others, such as the Crimean Tartars, who were moved eastwards by Stalin, want to return to their homelands. Even today some are not allowed to return and it is dangerous to protest too loudly. It must be remembered, however, that most Soviet citizens support their government and do not protest.

E The 15 Republics of the USSR

THE FIFTEEN REPUBLICS

1 Russian Soviet Federative Socialist Republic
2 Estonian Soviet Socialist Republic
3 Latvian SSR
4 Lithuanian SSR
5 Belorussian SSR
6 Ukrainian SSR
7 Moldavian SSR
8 Georgian SSR
9 Armenian SSR
10 Azerbaijan SSR
11 Kazakh SSR
12 Turkmen SSR
13 Uzbek SSR
14 Tajik SSR
15 Kirghiz SSR

Between 50 and 80 million of the 270 million Soviet citizens are religious. Religion is particularly strong among some of the national groups, for example the people of the five Central Asian republics are Moslem. There are also members of the Russian Orthodox Church, Catholics, Jews and Baptists in Russia. Communists do not believe in religion. Karl Marx warned:

❝ *It is the opium* (drug) *of the people.* ❞ (F)

Lenin added,

❝ *All modern religions and churches . . . serve to defend the exploitation of the people and stupefy the working class . . . Every religious idea, every idea of God, is unutterable vileness.* ❞ (G)

The Soviet Constitution allows people to believe in religion but not to teach or spread their religion. Khrushchev closed churches and places of worship. Such closures are now rare but attacks on religious beliefs continue. A few believers demand more freedom to practise their religion and they can end up in prison. One prisoner wrote:

❝ *Religious prisoners are extremely quiet and humble people, old men mainly . . . The prison authorities humiliated them in every possible way. Many believers had a rule that they must wear beards, yet they were all forcibly shaven while wearing handcuffs.* ❞ (H)

There are over two million Jews in Soviet Russia. Most of them seem content. Others want to go to Israel, the Jewish 'homeland'. In 1979 51 000 Jews were given exit visas but recently fewer have been allowed to leave – in 1984 it was only 897. The Soviet Government say that no more wanted to leave. But the names are known of 10 000 Jews who have been refused permission to emigrate. They are known as *Refuseniks*. Western experts think many more want to leave but are afraid to apply.

Life for Refuseniks is not easy. They are usually dismissed from their jobs and can then be arrested for being a 'parasite' (someone living off the work of others). In Moscow in 1985 a Jewish professor secretly told a BBC reporter,

❝ *Unfortunately, the situation in Jewish life here became worse than before; many are jailed – arrested, sentenced – for nothing, practically. Some of them are Hebrew teachers but, of course, they cannot officially be accused of studying Hebrew, so they are accused of many other things.* ❞ (J)

One such man is Yuli Edelstein. He was sent to prison because the KGB said they found drugs on a windowsill in his flat. Yuli protested – his flat has no windowsills.

In 1977 a new type of opposition appeared. A small group of workers formed The Free Trade Union to defend workers' rights. Many members have been beaten and arrested. All other trade unions are controlled by the government and do not protect workers.

???????????????

1 Explain the terms: dissidents; samizdat; refuseniks.

2 a Are **A** and **B** primary or secondary sources?
b How reliable are they as evidence about life in Soviet Russia?
c Who might consider these sources to be *biased* (one-sided)? Why?

3 a What do you think Karl Marx meant in **F**?
b In pairs, discuss what **G**, **H** and **J** tell you about the Soviet view of religion.

4 Imagine you are a reporter sent to interview Anatoly Marchenko. What questions would you like to ask him about life in Soviet Russia and in prison? What sort of answers might he give?

5 In groups, imagine you are dissidents living in Russia. You want to spread your ideas. How will you go about it? What problems might you face and how would you overcome them?

32 Conclusion: a Superpower with Problems

A Nikolai Gorbachev meets Prime Minister Margaret Thatcher on a visit to Britain in 1984

Mikhail Gorbachev (**A**) became the new Soviet leader in March 1985. He came from a younger generation than previous leaders, as *The Daily Telegraph* explained:

❝ *Mr Gorbachev is the youngest party leader since Stalin and the seventh since the 1917 Communist Revolution. He is the first party leader to have been born not only since the revolution but also since the death of Lenin.*

Mr Gorbachev is seen as a potential reformer with a more realistic view of the West than some others who might have been chosen. He was groomed by President Andropov as his preferred successor to lead Russia out of the sluggish era. ❞ (**B**)

(*Daily Telegraph*, 12 March 1985)

B and cartoon **C** suggest that Gorbachev, as a younger man, was expected to improve Russia's performance. He had a number of problems to deal with. Soviet foreign policy in the mid-1980s was bogged down. Soviet troops were still fighting in Afghanistan. Talks aimed at improving relations with China were making slow progress. Social unrest continued to simmer in Poland. Hopes for détente with America appeared slim.

At home the major problem remained poor economic performance. Gorbachev had to work out how to meet the demand for more consumer goods. The high birth rate among Moslems in Russia also caused Soviet leaders concern. By the year 2000, Moslems are expected to make up 25 per cent of the population. Few of them speak Russian and they are much closer in religion and culture to their neighbours in Iran and Afghanistan.

Watch out for news about Russia in newspapers and on television. How is the USSR trying to solve its problems at home and abroad? How successful are these attempts? What is likely to happen to relations with the West in the future?

How does life in Russia match up to your life in the West? Remember, the Russians place social facilities such as hospitals and old people's homes before the ownership of individual possessions. It may be very difficult to buy some goods, but essential foods such as bread and potatoes are cheap. Like the West, Russia is not a society of equals: there are, for example, special shops for Communist Party members to buy better quality goods. Remember, also, that Russians lack some freedoms you have in the West. Even so, the vast majority of Russian people are happy and proud of their country's achievements.

C Mr Gorbachev, in a *Daily Telegraph* cartoon